INSIDE CHURCHES

A Guide to Church Furnishings
Based on the original edition by Mrs Patricia Dirsztay

The National Association
of Decorative & Fine
Arts Societies

© National Association of Decorative and Fine Arts Societies 1989

First published in 1989 by Capability Publishing Ltd in association with
NADFAS Church Recorders
based on the original edition by Mrs Patricia Dirsztay.

The National Association of Decorative and Fine Arts Societies, 38 Ebury
Street, London SW1W 0LU

Capability Publishing Ltd, 629 Fulham Road,
London SW6 5UH

Designed by Red Kite Design Graphics

Printed in Clearface by BAS Printers Ltd,
Over Wallop, Hampshire

A CIP catalogue record for this book is available from the British Library

ISBN 0 - 9514062 - 0 - 5

Inside Churches has been compiled by the National Association of Decorative and Fine Arts Societies in conjunction with Capability Publishing Ltd., who would like to acknowledge with thanks, the generous help and advice of the following:

Michael Archer, Department of Ceramics, Victoria and Albert Museum; **David Beasley,** Deputy Librarian, Goldsmiths' Hall; **Jennifer Beazley,** Chairman, NADFAS Church Recorders; **Margaret Bell; John Blair,** The Queens College, Oxford; **Chris Blanchett,** Tiles and Architectural Ceramics Society; **Sheila Chapman,** Hon Secretary, NADFAS Church Recorders; **Pamela Clabburn,** Textile and embroidery consultant; **R.W.M. Clouston; Mrs Pamela Cowen,** Hon. Secretary, Heritage Co-ordination Group; **Mrs Patricia Dirsztay; Donald Findlay,** Council for the Care of Churches; **Phillippa Glanville,** Department of Metalwork, Victoria and Albert Museum; **Angela Goedicke,** Vice-Chairman, NADFAS Church Recorders; **Richard Grasby; Sarah Greenwood; Richard Hagen,** Furniture conservator; **Richard Harrison,** Director, Herbert Read Ltd, Ecclesiastical & Domestic Woodcarvers & Joiners; **Dr. Mary Hobbs,** Librarian, Chichester Cathedral Library; **Dr. Brian Kemp,** Church Monuments Society; **Patrick Moule,** British Institute of Organ Studies; **Nick Norman,** retired Master of the Royal Armories; **Dr. Tony North,** Department of Metalwork, Victoria and Albert Museum; **Tom Robinson,** Chairman, The Antiquarian Horological Society; **Richard Robson,** Curator, The Castle Howard Costume Galleries; **Elliott Viney,** Trustee, Patricia Fay Memorial Fund; **Lt. Col. J.F. Wilcox,** NADFAS Heraldry Adviser.

PREFACE

The Most Reverend Robert Runcie,
Archbishop of Canterbury

In my ministry as a bishop I have come to know and love two of the great Cathedrals of England - St. Albans and Canterbury. Yet my affection for the much humbler Oxfordshire parish church of Cuddesdon, where I was vicar, is just as deep. Our parish churches provide a very important record of past centuries of our Christian history, as well as being living witnesses to the Christian faith today. But their very familiarity tends to make us take them for granted.

This book will help us to avoid such complacency. It began life as a practical handbook for a group of people I have come to call the "shock troops" of church conservation - the Church Recorders of the National Association of Decorative and Fine Arts Societies. Over the years these groups of dedicated amateurs have been steadily building up a complete record and inventory of the interior details of many of Britain's parish churches. It is impossible to conserve what we do not know exists, so the Church Recorders have provided a vital key for later conservation. Records are deposited with the local parish and diocese, and with the Council for the Care of Churches and the Victoria and Albert Museum, providing an essential tool for the future protection and care of all those things which make churches such an important part of our local and national heritage.

By means of this book the NADFAS Church Recorders are making their specialist knowledge of churches available to us all. Consult this volume and you will be able to recognize, identify and date all the confusing objects which abound in church buildings. Like so many of the churches it explains, the book's simple arrangement belies the fascinating complexity of the information on offer. I frequently see visitors wandering aimlessly round a beautiful church, unable to comprehend the significance of the monuments, furniture and decorations around them. Now, with this book in hand, their visit might mean so much more.

There is another message in this book, perhaps a more significant one for the future. We are much more likely to protect the things we understand and to conserve that which we know. Readers of this book will, I believe, be motivated to preserve their local churches and, with them, so much of the history and past life of their communities. They will be helped to see the changes in the way we use church buildings in the present in the light of an understanding of the way they were used in the past. This will not prevent change but inform it, for conservation is not fossilisation. I hope this book will do almost as much as the work of the Church Recorders themselves in furthering an understanding of the great wealth Britain possesses in its parish churches, and in so doing contribute to the worship and life of the Church today.

J Robert Cantuar

CONTENTS

CONTENTS

CONTENTS

AN INTRODUCTION TO THE HISTORY OF THE CHURCH IN BRITAIN

Churches in Britain encapsulate much of the complex history of these islands. Nearly every town and village has its own parish church and most often it is the oldest building, set apart from the dwellings of ordinary people. Many churches are truly ancient, the first buildings in stone by early Christians, dating back to a time when religion was the main spring of society. It is not uncommon to find a church built by the Norman settlers of the 11th century but it is unusual for any church to date from only one century; many have something to offer from every period of our history. From the start, the shape, decoration and furnishings of our cathedrals and parish churches have been governed by the services held in them.

Although there has been a constant evolution over the centuries, we can recognise three distinct periods: the six hundred years to the Reformation in the mid-16th century; the next three hundred years during which a whole series of fundamental changes were followed by a period of stagnation; and finally, a re-awakening from the 1840's to today.

The Mediaeval Centuries

The entire mediaeval period was dominated by its religion and, in protestant times, it is easy to forget that mediaeval religion was an international one, based on a complex ritual centred on the Pope in Rome. Early churches were, therefore, Roman Catholic.

The Anglo-Saxons can have had few furnishings in their places of worship, apart from the cup used at Mass. From the earliest times, there would have been a font for baptism and, because it is usually free-standing, the font has often survived from Norman times even if the church around it has been entirely rebuilt. The Normans built many small stone 3 or 4 cell churches with a small chancel and a slightly larger nave. In the earliest, processions around a tomb of a saint or bishop were an essential part of ritual and a rounded apse at the east end of the church provided space. As churches increased in size, the aisles took over this function and the east end tended to be flattened.

The 11th and 12th centuries were the great period of monasticism. Many churches were bequeathed by their lay patrons to a wealthy cathedral or abbey. From earliest times, the chancel had been the responsibility of the priest and the nave of the parish. With the appointment of church wardens from 1129, the laiety had more influence on changes in the main body of the church. The patronage of wealthy benefactors encouraged a proliferation of new aisles, steeples, porches, towers and clerestory windows all of which fundamentally affected the appearance of the church.

The 12th and 13th centuries saw a period of remarkable decorative innovation. Perhaps the most significant was the arrival of stained glass, in cathedrals from the 1170's and in parish churches in the 13th century. At the same time wall paintings began to appear, covering the nave walls with biblical scenes and always focussed on the great Doom or Day of Judgement over the chancel arch and above the rood. In the 13th century mass would have been said daily. A traveller entering the south door would have first seen the figure of St Christopher painted on the opposite wall. The single Sanctus bell would have told him that the service was starting; it would have rung again at the Elevation of the Host. Mass could only be said once daily at any particular altar, so as the number of priests grew, it became necessary to have additional altars, often placed at the east end of the side-aisles, so that separate chapels within the main body of the church were formed.

Not many mediaeval churches had pulpits. Preaching was more often done by friars at the village cross which could be in the churchyard or on the village green. In the 13th century, fonts were covered to protect the consecrated water from theft. It seems that the consecrated water was seldom changed.

Memorials began to appear. For centuries they were confined to the graves of priests and great men. At first, even the grandest had only a simple cross incised on their tomb slabs. These developed into figures of recumbent knights and ladies, first in stone and then in alabaster. The less ambitious or those who could not afford a massive stone or marble monument were content with a decorated brass memorial. The earliest brass in England is dated 1277 and they continued to be popular until the early 17th century.

The Black Death, or bubonic plague, that swept the country in the mid-14th century was a social and economic disaster but it had another long term effect in encouraging a general acceptance of the uncertainty of life and an increasing concern for the after-life. The wealthy began to build chantry chapels, endowing them with a priest to pray perpetually for their souls. The obsession with death can be seen in the skulls and skeletons carved into monuments.

In the century before the Reformation, there was much rebuilding, particularly in the counties which prospered from the wool trade, but everywhere towers were being added to the west end of churches. These were principally to house a set of bells, but there was undoubtedly rivalry between neighbouring parishes to build the grandest or the highest tower. Two other developments mark the 15th century. The introduction of simple benches for seating and the substitution of the old steep pitched roof by a flatter one which made possible the insertion of a new tier of clerestory windows high above the nave.

The Anglican Church

The Reformation of the 1530's transferred supreme authority from the Pope to the English monarch following which the Church of England gradually emerged, beginning with the Acts of Supremacy and Uniformity in 1559, the Articles of Religion in 1571 and culminating in the Book of Common Prayer as part of the Restoration Settlement in 1662. Arising from these changes the interior and fittings of all churches were fundamentally altered. An obsession against any form of idolatry meant the destruction or mutilation of statues, fonts and tombs, the removal of much stained glass, the obliteration of wall paintings and the removal of the Rood, whilst stone altars were replaced by plain wood tables. Initially plate, vestments and altar hangings were confiscated to be replaced gradually over the next three hundred years.

To accommodate the changed needs of the changed liturgy, in the 17th century, a number of new furnishings appeared. The new Anglican service emphasised Mattins and Evensong so the Eucharist or communion mass became an occasional service. Since preaching was the most important element of the service, for the next two hundred years, the pulpit was the dominant feature in most churches. Pulpits were set high because they had to place the preacher above the new box pews and the tester above helped to carry the preacher's words to the ends of the church.

Other innovations of these years were the Poorbox and the Breadbasket for the distribution of alms to the poor, based on the mediaeval monastic system of Bread Dole. The display of The Sentences (Lord's Prayer, Creed and Ten Commandments) was made obligatory in churches in 1603 and the Royal Arms, signifying the monarch as Head of the Church became a universal ornament after 1662. In the 1630's, Archbishop Laud introduced altar rails to prevent dogs from approaching the Table.

Almost no new churches were built between the Reformation and the Great Fire of London after which a radically different style of church design appeared, classical in form and planned to accommodate the contemporary liturgy. Architects like Wren, Hawksmoor and Gibbs saw churches as preaching boxes, rectangular halls with galleries, plain glass in round-headed windows, no east window but a reredos behind the altar, probably incorporating the Sentences, box pews and a dominating pulpit. Magnificent new plate was donated by patrons and, in country churches, hatchments were set high on the walls when the local squire died. This was the great age of English sculpture and magnificent, but often overlarge, monuments filled the chancel.

The Victorian Revival and After

The Church of England dozed through the late 18th and early 19th centuries, leaving churches generally damp, decaying and uncared for until the electric impact of the Oxford Movement in the 1840's jerked the Church out of its inertia. With the Ecclesiologists in command, there began a revolution which, in 30 years, restored or built the majority of parish churches, saving many from total decay but destroying or distorting much of beauty and antiquity in the process. A reaction against the Carolean and Georgian periods meant the loss of box pews and many pulpits and the removal of classical monuments to more obscure parts of the building. The musicians in the west gallery were replaced by a surpliced choir in the chancel backed by an organ. There were new brass lecterns, altarcloths, vestments, new tiles on the floor and new stained glass (of very varying quality) in the windows. Pulpits were rebuilt in stone and fonts, which had become much smaller after the Reformation when total immersion at baptism ceased, returned to their mediaeval size.

There have been changes enough since then. Today's churches offer us a mix and amalgam of all periods and architectural styles. Search for it and there is evidence to be found of every period of the church's gradual evolution. Radical changes in belief and liturgy produced sudden new directions. We can trace them through the objects, decoration and furnishings they left behind. It is the sheer variety of Britain's churches and the historical breadth that they incorporate that combines to ensure their perennial fascination.

How to Use This Guide

Inside Churches is a practical reference book. It will help you to name and identify the furnishings of any parish church or cathedral in Britain.
This is how it works....

At the front is a **general introduction** to the history of the church in Britain from earliest times until today. The book is organised in three overall sections:

Styles and Terminology chapters will tell you HOW to describe the things you see
Materials chapters will tell you WHAT you see depending whether it is made of wood, metal, paper, cloth or stone
Objects chapters will tell you WHAT it is if it falls into a one of several special categories, eg. musical instruments.

Within each section are **chapters** covering different aspects to help you increase your knowledge and understanding. In turn within each chapter are different **sub-sections** dealing with specific groups of styles or objects.

If, for example, you are looking at a piece of furniture. Is it made of wood? Turn to the WOOD chapter. At the beginning of the chapter you find a glossary of the special terms used to describe types of wood and types of decoration and construction specific to this material. If your piece of furniture looks like a table, turn to the sub-section TABLES. Does it look like any of the illustrated examples? If so, you will find either its name and, perhaps, date or even a full description of it using the correct terms. If you can find no similar illustration, turn back to the front of the chapter to identify its constituent parts (legs, feet and backs give the most clues). In all cases, the chapters in the first section STYLES AND TERMINOLOGY will help you describe and interpret the decoration or any object you find difficult to identify. At some point in your search through the book, you will have found out exactly what it is, what it was used for, approximately how old it might be and how to describe it.

If you already know what the object is but want to learn more, or if you come across a term that is unfamiliar, turn to the **Index** in the back of the book.

Throughout the text, proper names are in highlighted thus   **Credence:**
        descriptions are in roman type, thus   of trestle form;
        and explanations are in italic type, thus   *(sanctuary table).*

Description is important to **Inside Churches** because the book's primary aim is to help people record the objects and decoration in churches, which form part of our heritage. If you are a CHURCH RECORDER you will find notes in italics at the foot of those sections where particular recording techniques are advised. In general, however, you will need to describe the object in detail noting decoration, colour, position, inscriptions or maker's name and its state of preservation. Add photographs and sketch drawings where you can.

If you want more information on Church Recorders, write to:

Church Recorders, The National Association of Decorative and Fine Arts Societies, 38 Ebury Street, London SW1W 0LU.

Inside Churches will give you an introduction to a wide number of decorative and fine arts and help increase your knowledge of church interiors. However, it would not be practical to answer all your questions, so if you want to know more about any particular aspect, turn to **Further Reading** for a selection of reference books.

STYLES & TERMINOLOGY

ARCHITECTURE
Terms

The main decorative periods of British Church Art and Architecture:

600-1066	Saxon
1066-1199	Norman
1170-1300	Early English ⎫
1272-1349	Decorated ⎬ Gothic
1350-1539	Perpendicular ⎭
1485-1689	Renaissance
1485-1603	Tudor
1558-1603	Elizabethan
1603-1640	Early Stuart/Jacobean
1640 -1660	Cromwellian/Puritan
1660-1700	Restoration/Carolean/Baroque
1700-1770	Queen Anne/ Georgian
1760-1800	Rococo/ Gothick revival
1800-1820	Regency/ Classical Revival
1837-1900	Victorian
1860-1900	Pre-Raphaelite
1890-1915	Art Nouveau/ Arts and Crafts
1920-1936	Art Deco
1950-	Modern

THE CHURCH

Christian Churches are most often cruciform in shape with the altar at the Eastern end.

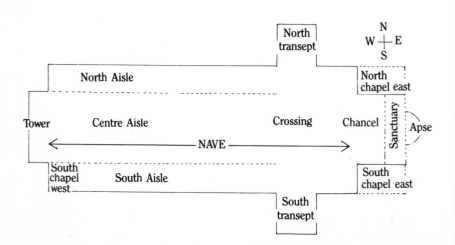

2

ABACUS
The slab on top of a **capital** on which the **architrave** rests; the shape varies according to the **Order**.

Lugged or eared architrave

ARCHITRAVE
The moulded frame surrounding a door or window. It is also the lowest main division of the **entablature**, between the **frieze** and **abacus**. A **lintel** is the horizontal member over a door or window.

CORNICE
The uppermost member of an entablature, surmounting the frieze, or any moulded projection which crowns the part to which it is fixed, e.g. wall, door, column, piece of furniture, window, panelling, etc.

FRIEZE
A decorative band between the architrave and **cornice** or, in furniture, between the cornice and framework.

IMPOST
The slab, usually moulded, on which the ends of an **arch** rest.

PEDIMENT
An ornamental low pitched triangular or segmented **gable** above the cornice of an entablature.

Triangular

Segmented

Swan-necked

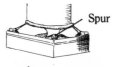

Broken

Open

Scrolled

Spur

SPUR
An ornamental protrusion on the corner between the base of a **column** or **pillar** and the **plinth**. Also a fixed draught **screen**, or a **buttress**.

TYMPANUM The filled-in space of a pediment or of the curved section of an arch.

ARCHITECTURE
Terms

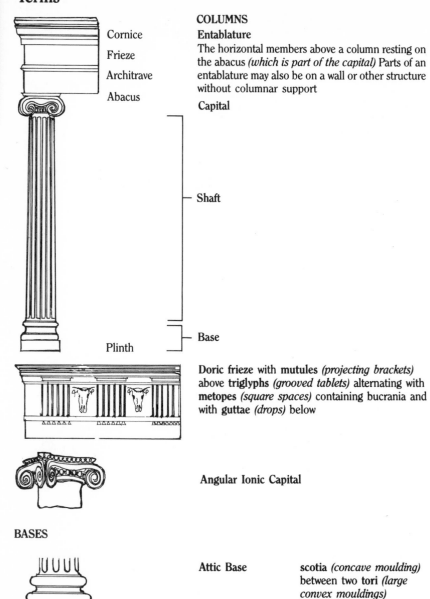

Cornice

Frieze

Architrave

Abacus

Shaft

Base

Plinth

COLUMNS

Entablature
The horizontal members above a column resting on the abacus *(which is part of the capital)* Parts of an entablature may also be on a wall or other structure without columnar support

Capital

Doric frieze with **mutules** *(projecting brackets)* above **triglyphs** *(grooved tablets)* alternating with **metopes** *(square spaces)* containing bucrania and with **guttae** *(drops)* below

Angular Ionic Capital

BASES

Attic Base	**scotia** *(concave moulding)* between two **tori** *(large convex mouldings)*
Tuscan Base	torus with a fillet above
Base	with two **astragals** *(small convex moulding)* with a scotia above and a torus below

4

ARCHITECTURE
Columns and Supports

The term "column" describes a pillar of any one of the five classical Orders. Supports deviating in shape from the Orders have other names. Greek and Roman Orders differ slightly.

DORIC is distinguished by triglyphs and metopes in the frieze and mutules under the corona.
Greek Doric has a fluted shaft and no base.
Roman Doric has a base and fluted or plain shaft

IONIC has volutes on the capital and dentils in the cornice, the shaft is usually fluted and the base, "attic"

CORINTHIAN has a fluted shaft, a capital ornamented with acanthus, olive or laurel leaves and eight small volutes

TUSCAN is simplified Doric

COMPOSITE is an ornate version of Corinthian and occurs in various forms

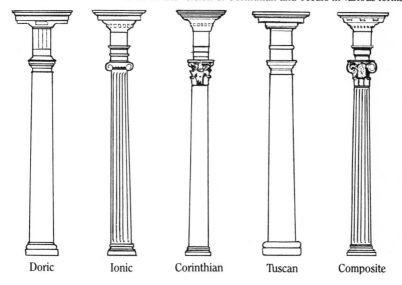

| Doric | Ionic | Corinthian | Tuscan | Composite |

OTHER CAPITALS

Cushion
Norman

Scalloped
Norman

Waterleaf
12th century

Crocket or Volute
Transitional

Stiff Leaf
13th century

Natural Leaf
14th century

5

ARCHITECTURE
Columns and Supports

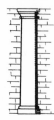

Engaged Column

Lesene or Pilaster Strip
thin pilaster without base or capital

Colonettes
diminutive columns

Compound Pier

Pillar
solid detached upright support, deviating in shape and proportion from the Orders

Pillar of clustered shafts
(often misnamed as a clustered column)

Blind Arcade

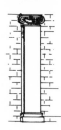

Pilaster *rectangular support projecting slightly from a surface, with base and capital*

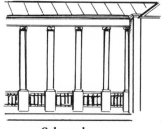

Colonnade

SAXON 7th CENTURY - 1066
Few, very plain mouldings; and massive impost blocks

NORMAN 1066-1200
Has some plain mouldings, but many richly carved. The chief characteristic is a series of concentric rings, each one projecting more than the one under it. Beakheads and chevron are popular motifs. The top edge of the abacus is generally squared and the capitals cushioned, scalloped or volute.

EARLY ENGLISH (GOTHIC) 1200-1300
Has mouldings of deeply cut rounds and hollows, a rounded abacus and dogtooth and stiff leaf ornament. Shafts are round and at times clustered and arches acutely pointed or trefoil.
(For Foils and Cusps see WINDOWS)

DECORATED (GOTHIC) 1300-50
Has numerous lightly cut mouldings with ogee curves. The abacus is absorbed into the capital and composed of three members with ornament between rolls of moulding. Crockets and pinnacles abound.

PERPENDICULAR (GOTHIC) 1350-1660
Has less pointed arches, some segmented or flat headed, wide and shallow mouldings which are sometimes carried right round the arch down to the floor. Ornament of scroll, ballflower, fourleaf and naturalistic foliage, Tudor rose and Tudor flower and much brattishing.

RENAISSANCE 1603-89
Style based on the antique classical orders with round arches and piers.

CLASSICAL 1689-1837
Style based on the antique classical orders incorporating putti and garlands in the decoration.

ARCHITECTURE
Arches

AEDICULE
A classical architectural surround to an opening *(door, window, niche, etc.)* of columns or pillars and a pediment or entablature.

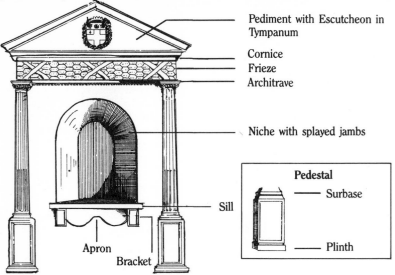

Pediment with Escutcheon in Tympanum

Cornice
Frieze
Architrave

Niche with splayed jambs

Sill

Apron
Bracket

Pedestal
— Surbase

— Plinth

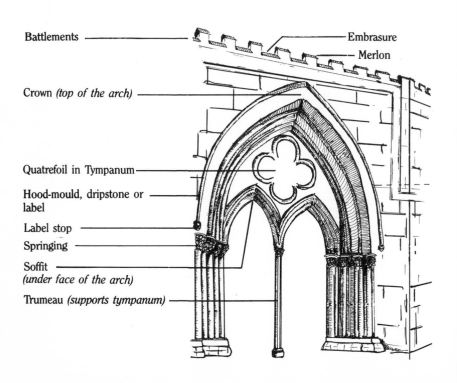

Battlements

Embrasure
Merlon

Crown *(top of the arch)*

Quatrefoil in Tympanum

Hood-mould, dripstone or label

Label stop

Springing

Soffit
(under face of the arch)

Trumeau *(supports tympanum)*

ARCHITECTURE
Arches

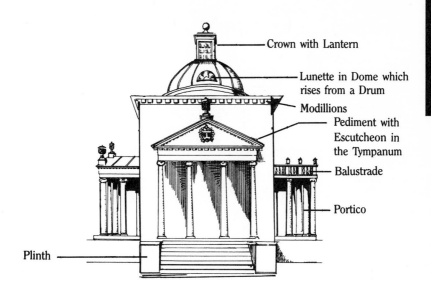

Crown with Lantern

Lunette in Dome which rises from a Drum

Modillions

Pediment with Escutcheon in the Tympanum

Balustrade

Portico

Plinth

ARCADE A series of arches supported on piers or columns.

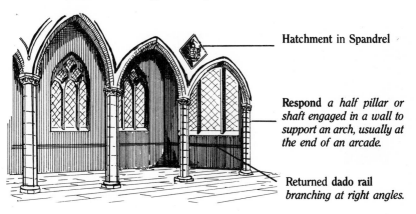

Hatchment in Spandrel

Respond *a half pillar or shaft engaged in a wall to support an arch, usually at the end of an arcade.*

Returned **dado rail** *branching at right angles.*

Acroterion ornament at apex or lower angles of pediment
Stylobate basement supporting columns or pillars

9

ARCHITECTURE
Roofs

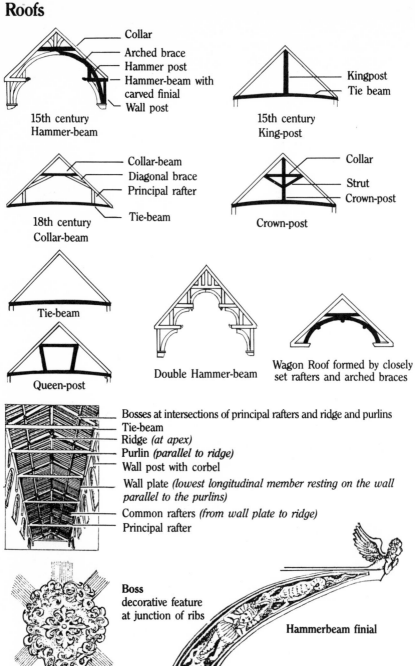

Collar
Arched brace
Hammer post
Hammer-beam with carved finial
Wall post

15th century
Hammer-beam

Kingpost
Tie beam

15th century
King-post

Collar-beam
Diagonal brace
Principal rafter

18th century
Collar-beam

Tie-beam

Collar
Strut
Crown-post

Crown-post

Tie-beam

Queen-post

Double Hammer-beam

Wagon Roof formed by closely set rafters and arched braces

Bosses at intersections of principal rafters and ridge and purlins
Tie-beam
Ridge *(at apex)*
Purlin *(parallel to ridge)*
Wall post with corbel
Wall plate *(lowest longitudinal member resting on the wall parallel to the purlins)*
Common rafters *(from wall plate to ridge)*
Principal rafter

Boss
decorative feature
at junction of ribs

Hammerbeam finial

The sanctuary is the centrepoint of the church, although its arrangement is not strictly architectural much architectural terminology is used to describe the formal arrangement of objects in the sanctuary. The arrangement will differ according to the form of the service. In Anglican churches, the Sacrament will generally be kept in an aumbry or hanging pyx. In Roman Catholic churches, the Sacrament is generally kept in a tabernacle on the altar.

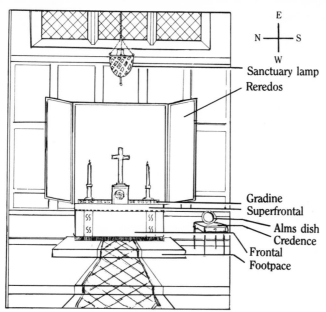

Altar	stone or wooden table or purpose built frame
Antependium	carved or painted moveable panel of wood or metal serving as altar facade
Aumbry	cupboard, usually for sacred vessels, in north wall of chancel
Credence	serving table on S side of altar
Footpace	step on which altar stands, returning to East wall rather than running across church
Frontal	textile forming facade of altar
Gradine	shelf at rear of altar-top and step on which altar stands
Laudian	loose throw-over altar covering reaching ground on all sides
Reredos	screen covering wall behind and above altar. If it is a curtain, it is known as a **dossal**; if a painting, it is an **altarpiece**; if a hinged painting or panel it is a **diptych** or **triptych** retable.
Super frontal	band, usually fringed, sometimes contrasting, overlapping top of frontal
Tabernacle	receptacle for the Reserved Sacrament, which may hang from the ceiling and be covered by a veil

ATTRIBUTES AND ALLEGORY
Saints

Biblical stories in stained glass, monumental carvings and painted scenes had to be understood by people who could not read. Through the mediaeval period a complex iconography developed linking every saint, apostle or biblical personality with an image which identified him with the event that gave him prominence. Today, these images are often incomprehensible because we no longer understand the references.

SAINTS' ATTRIBUTES
Images of Saints were easily identified by mediaeval people by the symbols or attributes they carried. A woman holding a wheel, for example, is probably Catherine of Alexandria who was martyred on a wheel.

Attributes often appear in combinations, which will help clear up confusion between saints with similar attributes. A fallen dragon, for example, could indicate any one of several saints. If the figure is winged, it must be St Michael the Archangel. If it is a dragon being speared by a figure on a white horse, the saint depicted is St George. If, on the other hand, the figure is female and positioned above or rising out of the dragon's belly, it must be Margaret of Antioch. But it would be Martha if the female figure held an aspergillum since she disposed of her dragon by sprinkling it with holy water. However, saints are not always shown with all possible attributes, sometimes one and sometimes another will give the necessary identification.

Saints are listed first by attribute and then by name. Their accustomed dress is not strictly an attribute, but is included as one where appropriate since it may be an important identifiyng characteristic.

Beast and Men

Cow	Bridgit of Kildare	Lion & raven	Vincent
		Lion (winged)	Mark
Dog	Roch, with plague sore on leg	Man (winged)	Matthew
Dogs (2)	Dominic, with black and white dogs holding torches in mouths	Mule (kneeling)	Anthony of Padua
		Otter	Bishop Cuthbert
		Ox (winged)	Luke
Dragon & cross	Margaret of Antioch	Oxen (2)	Walstan, who also holds a scythe
Dragon led by chain	Juliana of Nicanedia	Pig, boar or hog	Anthony of Egypt (Anthony Abbot)
Dragon	Archangel Michael (winged); George, usually in armour, or Martha	Sheep	Genevieve
		Stag (with crucifix between horns)	Eustace or Hubert,
Horse, white	George		
Lamb	Agnes; Francis of Assisi; John the Baptist	Wolf (guarding head)	Edmund
		Wolf, Lion or Cock	Vitus
Lion	Euphemia or Jerome		

Birds

Birds	Francis of Assisi
Cock	Peter
Cock, lion or wolf	Vitus
Does (2)	Withburga
Dove	Pope Gregory
Dove on sceptre	King Edmund
Dove on shoulder	David of Wales
Doves in cage or basket (2)	Joseph or Joachim
Eagle	John the Evangelist
Partridge	Jerome
Swan & flowers	Hugh of Lincoln

Objects and Flowers

Anchor	Clement or Bishop Nicholas
Anvil	Adrian or Bishop Eloi
Armour (trampling on devil)	Michael
Armour (white horse with dragon)	George
Arrow (piercing breast or hand)	Giles
Arrow (piercing crown)	Edmund
Arrows (pierced by and bound to tree)	Sebastian (naked)
Axe	Matthias
Bag of money	Matthew
Balls (3)	Nicholas
Banner (red cross & surrounded by virgins)	Ursula
Basket of fruit & flowers	Dorothea/Dorothy
Basket or pitcher	Zita
Basket with loaves	Philip
Beehive	Ambrose; Bernard of Clairvaux; John Chrysostom
Beggar	Edith of Wilton (washing feet of beggar)
Beggar (receiving cloak)	Martin
Bell	Anthony Abbot
Bones	Ambrose
Book	many saints hold a gospel
Book & crook	Chad
Books	Ambrose or Boniface
Bottle	James the Great
Box or vase (alabaster)	Mary Magdalene (with long hair)
Breasts, on plate	Agatha
Candle (devil blowing it out)	Genevieve
Capstan	Erasmus, Bishop of Formiae or Elmo
Cauldron of oil	Vitus
Chains	Leonard
Child on arm	Anthony of Padua
Child Jesus on shoulder	Christopher (crossing river)
Child, crucified	William of Norwich
Children carried (2)	Eustace
Children in tub (3)	Nicholas
Children, male (2)	Mary, wife of Cleophas
Church (model of)	Withburga (2 does at feet) or Botolph or other founder
Cloth (imprinted with face of Christ)	Veronica
Comb (iron)	Bishop Blaise
Cross (inverted)	Peter
Cross (red on white)	George
Cross (saltire)	Andrew
Crown of roses	Cecilia
Crown of roses or holding roses	Dorothy or Teresa
Demon at feet	Norbert (in white habit)
Devil trampled on by man in armour	Michael
Devil with bellows	Genevieve
Drug jars	Cosmas and Damian

13

ATTRIBUTES & ALLEGORY
Saints

Eyes on dish	Lucy	Clairvaux
		Luke
	Picture of Virgin	
Flame in hand or breast	Anthony of Padua	Pincers	Agatha; Dunstan; Apollonia (holding tooth)
Gridiron	Laurence or Vincent	Pot of holy water & ladle	Martha
		Saw	Simon
Halberd	Jude	Scallop shell	James the Great
Head (own, carried before altar)	Winefred or Osyth	Scourge	Ambrose
		Scythe and carrying head	Sidwell or Sithewell
Head (own, crowned and carried)	Bishop Cuthbert or Bishop Denis	Scythe and oxen (2)	Walstan
Head (man's under feet)	Catherine of Alexandria	Set-square	Thomas
		Shears	Agatha
Heart (flaming or transfixed by sword)	Augustine of Hippo	Sieve (broken)	Benedict
		Staff	James the Great; James the Less; Bridget of Sweden or Anthony Abbot
Hermit	Anthony Abbot		
Horseshoe	Eloi		
Idols (broken)	Wilfrid (baptising pagans)	Stone (striking head)	Stephen
		Sword	Paul or Barbara
		Sword through breast	Euphemia
Keys	Peter; Zita; Martha (at girdle)	Sword through neck	Lucy
Knife & skin over arm	Bartholomew	T-cross	Philip
		T-cross on shoulder	Anthony Abbot
		Together	Cosmas & Damian; Raphael & Tobias (carrying fish); Peter & Paul; Philip & James
Lily	Euphemia; Joseph; Dominic (in black habit); Catherine of Sienna		
Loaves	Olaf or Zita	Tower	Barbara
Loaves & fishes	disciples	Tree	Etheldreda (asleep)
		Tree (under foot)	Bishop Boniface
		True Cross	Helen
Manacles	Leonard (holding them)		
Medical equipment	Cosmas and Damian	Weighing souls	Michael
		Wheel	Catherine of Alexandria (man's head under feet)
Millstone	Vincent		
Musical instruments	Cecilia		Matthew
		Winged man	
Olive branch	Agnes	Wounded forehead (red band)	Bridget of Sweden
Pagans being baptised	Wilfrid	Wounded leg	Roch (also with angel, dog, staff or shell)
Palm	Agnes or other martyr		
		Wounds of Christ (**stigmata**)	Francis of Assisi
Peacock feather	Barbara		
Pen, ink & scroll	Mark; Matthew; Bernard of Clairvaux		

SAINTS AND APOSTLES
Saints

Apostles are marked ★, there are always 12, but not always the same saints. Jude, Simon and Matthias are not always included. Apostles may also carry scrolls which contain the creed. The principal attribute of each saint is highlighted.

Adrian	**anvil**; axe; sword
Agatha	**dish containing her breasts**; pincers; shears
Agnes	olive branch; **lamb**; palm
Aidan	stag at feet; **flaming torch**
Alban	**sword**; fountain; his head in his hands; mace
Alphege	chasuble full of stones
Ambrose	**beehive**; books; 2 human bones; scourge with 3 knots
★Andrew	saltire cross
Anthony Abbot	bell; pig; fire; **stick with T-shaped handle**; Tau cross on shoulder of cloak
Anthony of Padua	**Franciscan habit**; infant Christ in arms; flame in hand or on breast; kneeling mules
Apollonia	pincers holding tooth
Augustine of Canterbury	dressed as archbishop
Augustine of Hippo	dressed as bishop; books; **flaming heart transfixed by 2 arrows**
Barbara	cup and wafer; **tower**; feather; sword; crown
★Barnabas	Tudor roses on shield or gospel
★Bartholomew	**Knife**, his skin held over his arm
Benedict	**Benedictine habit** (black or white of the reformed order); broken cup; sprinkler; raven with loaf in beak; broken sieve
Bernard of Clairvaux	**white habit with pastoral staff**; beehive; inkhorn; pen; 3 mitres; bound dragon
Blaise	dressed as bishop; **iron comb**
Boniface	dressed as archbishop; **book transfixed by sword** or stained with blood; foot on tree
Botolph	dressed as abbot
Bridget of Sweden	**taper or candle**; crozier; staff; red band across forehead
Catherine of Alexandria	**wheel**; head of man under feet
Catherine of Sienna	white tunic and veil with black cloak; **cross with lily**; book or rosary in hands
Cecilia	crown of roses; **musical instruments**
Chad	book and crook; **St. Chad's cross**
Christopher	carrying infant Christ across river
Clare	dressed as nun; cross; lily; **pyx or monstrance**
Clement	dressed as Pope or bishop; **anchor**
Cosmas & Damian	always together; dressed as physicians (dark red robes lined with fur); **medical equipment**
Cuthbert	dressed as bishop; otter; **St Oswald's crowned head in hands**
David of Wales	dressed as bishop; bible; **dove on shoulder**
Denis	dressed as bishop; carries his own head
Dominic	black and white habit; **black and white dogs with torch in mouth**; star on forehead; lily

Dorothea/Dorothy	basket of roses; roses and apples; crown of roses
Dunstan	**gold cup on blue field**; red hot pincers
Edith of Wilton	washing feet of beggar
Edmund	dressed as king; **crown pierced by arrows**; wolf guarding head; arrow
Edward	dressed as king; sceptre surmounted by dove; ring
Elizabeth	mother of John the Baptist in Salutation scenes
Eloi or Eligius	dressed as bishop; hammer and tongs; **anvil**; horseshoe; bellows at feet
Erasmus	dressed as bishop; **capstan**; sailing ship
Etheldreda	dressed as nun; crowned; building church; asleep under tree
Euphemia	**sword through breast**; lion; bear; lily
Eustace	**stag with crucifix between horns**; carrying 2 children across river; brass bull
Francis of Assisi	birds; lamb; lily; stigmata
Friedesweida	dressed as abbess, crowned; gospels
Genevieve	dressed as nun; devil blowing out lighted candle relit by angel; **crook or distaff**; sheep; basket of loaves
George	red cross on white ground on banner or breast; white horse; dragon
Giles	arrow piercing hand and stag; **hind pierced by arrow**
Gregory	dressed as pope; dove on shoulder; dove hovering overhead
Helena	dressed as empress; large cross (True cross)
Hubert	dressed as hunter or bishop; stag with crucifix between horns, beside him or crouched on book
Hugh of Lincoln	Carthusian habit; **swan**; 3 flowers
Ives or Yvo	dressed as lawyer; surrounded by widows and orphans
★James the Great	**scallop shell**; staff; bottle; pilgrim's broad-brimmed hat
★James the Less	**fuller's staff** or club
Jerome	cardinal's hat; lion; portrayed as man of learning at desk
Joachim	meeting St Anne at gate; basket with 2 doves
John Chrysostom	beehive; **dove at ear**; chalice; gospels
John de Matha	white habit with blue/red cross on breast; fetters; angels leading captives
John the Baptist	lamb; tall staff with cross piece; hairy coat
★John the Evangelist	eagle; cup with serpent
Joseph	lily
Joseph of Arimathaea	shroud; crown of thorns; nails
★Jude	**halberd**; club; lance
Julian	blue saltire cross on silver
Juliana of Nicanedia	**devil flogged** or held in chains
Laurence	gridiron
Leonard	dressed as deacon or abbot; holding chains; manacles; **broken fetters**
Louis IX	dressed as king or Franciscan; **crown of thorns**; 3 nails of the cross

Lucy	eyes in dish; sword; wound in neck
★Luke the Evangelist	ox; picture of Virgin Mary
Margaret of Antioch	rising from belly of dragon; dragon; palm; cross
★Mark the Evangelist	lion; pen; ink; scroll
Martha	keys at girdle; trampling dragon; aspergillum; ladle
Martin	giving half cloak to beggar or cripple; dressed as bishop; goose at feet
Mary, wife of Cleophas	4 sons (James, John, Simon, Joseph) & their attributes
Mary Magdalene	alabaster vase or box; long blonde hair
★Matthew the Evangelist	winged man; ink; scroll; pen; bag of money; knife; dagger
★Matthias	axe; halberd
Nicholas	dressed as bishop; ship; anchor; 3 golden balls or purses; 3 children in tub
Norbert	dressed in white habit over black; devil bound at feet; spider in chalice; monstrance or ciborium
Olaf	loaves
Oswald	dressed as king; sceptre; cross; silver dish
Osyth or Sytha	dressed as queen or abbess; own head in hands
★Paul	sword;
★Peter	keys; fish; inverted cross; beard; curly hair
Peter the Martyr	dressed as Dominican; wound in head
★Philip	cross; T-shaped cross; basket of loaves
Radegunda	dressed as abbess (crowned); kneeling captive at feet; holding broken fetters
Roch	pointing at plague sore on leg; staff; shell; dog; angel
Sebastian	bound to tree or column; pierced by arrows
Sidwell or Sithewell	scythe; well; head in hands
★Simon	fishes; saw; cross
Stephen	dressed as deacon; stone striking head
Swithin	dressed as bishop (Winchester)
Sylvester	dressed as pope; bound; 2 dead pagans; spear; dagger
Teresa of Avila	dressed in brown habit; roses; dragon
★Thomas	builder's set-square; ruler; girdle
Thomas a Becket	dressed as archbishop or Benedictine; wound in head
Thomas Aquinas	dressed as Dominican; star on breast
Ursula	arrow in hand; banner (red cross on white)
Veronica	cloth marked with head of Christ in hand
Vincent	dressed as deacon; raven; gridiron; millstone; whip in hand
Vitus	cauldron of oil; boy with palm; cock; lion; wolf

ATTRIBUTES & ALLEGORY

ATTRIBUTES & ALLEGORY
Saints

Walstan	crowned; scythe in hand; 2 oxen at feet
Wilfrid	baptising pagans; broken idols
William of Norwich	child crucified; cross and nails; hammer and nails
Winefred	own head in hands before altar; sword; palm branch; book
Withburga	2 does at feet; church in hand
Wulfstan, Wulstan or Wolstan	dressed as bishop; fixing crozier in tomb (of St Edmund); devil with book; giving sight to blind man
Zita, Citha or Sitha	dressed as housekeeper; keys; loaves; rosary; bag; pitcher; basket

EVANGELISTS

As saints, the four gospel writers may have several attributes, but where they are given prominence as evangelists one only is usual.

Matthew	Mark	Luke	John
winged man	winged lion	winged ox	eagle

ANGELIC ORDERS
Archangels

Gabriel	Annunciation
Michael	Last Judgement or killing dragon
Raphael	with Tobias and fish
Uriel	
Angels	one pair of wings; halo; holding scrolls, instruments of the Passion or musical instruments
Cherubim and Seraphim	6 wings; wings may be strewn with eyes; may be depicted as warriors or judges
Thrones	scarlet wheels with wings, sometimes strewn with eyes
Prophets	Amos, Daniel, Ezekiel, Habakkuk, Haggai, Hosea, Isaiah, Jeremiah, Joel, Jonah, Malachi, Micah, Nahum, Obadiah, Zechariah, Zephaniah

LATIN DOCTORS

The mediaeval church recognised 4 principal scholars of the church.

Augustine	dressed as bishop or doctor
Ambrose	dressed as bishop
Gregory	dressed as pope
Jerome	dressed as cardinal

ATTRIBUTES & ALLEGORY

18

HOLY ORDERS

Each of the Holy Orders has its own characteristic dress or habit. Saints who were also monks or prelates are often depicted wearing the dress of their order or rank.

Benedictine	black habit *Benedict; Boniface; Thomas à Becket*
Carmelite	white cloak over brown habit (since 1297) *John de Matha, with blue/red cross on breast, fetters or angel leading captives*
Carthusian	white habit *Hugh of Lincoln, with swan and 3 flowers*
Cistercian	white or grey habit *Bernard of Clairvaux, with 3 crowns*
Dominican	white tunic, black cloak with hood *Dominic, with star on forehead and 2 dogs carrying torches; Peter the Martyr, with wound in head; Thomas Aquinas, with chalice and star on breast*
Franciscan	brown or grey habit *Francis of Assisi, with birds or animals; Anthony of Padua, with infant Christ; Louis IX, with crown of thorns*
Knights Templar	white wool habit with red cross
Knights of St John	long wide black tunic with white cross on breast (red surcoat for high ranks)
Martyrs	palm
Hermits	t-shaped staff; rosary
Pilgrims	hat with shell; staff; wallet
Founders	model of church or monastery in hand
Abbots and Bishops	pastoral staff or crozier
Archbishops	dressed in pall *Boniface; Augustine of Canterbury; Thomas à Becket*
Popes	triple tiara; cope; pallium; triple cross in hand
Cardinals	red hat; red cloak; red robe *Jerome*

KINGS

Kings and Queens are usually richly dressed and crowned
Kings
Edmund; Oswald; Louis IX
Queens
Helen; Friedesweide; Elizabeth of Hungary
Emperor
holding imperial standard, bearing cross and Chi Rho symbol (labarum)
Constantine

ATTRIBUTES & ALLEGORY
The Bible

BIBLICAL SCENES
Certain scenes, stories and themes from the Bible are often represented, sometimes with titles. There are many variations, but some of the commonest scenes described in a series of respresentations are indicated here.

Types and Antitypes
Types *(Old Testament incidents)* are often balanced by or used to forshadow **antitypes** *(New Testament incidents)* in Christian decoration. Jonah was trapped in the whale for 3 days, for example, the same period of time as Christ's entombment, and the two scenes often appear together to symbolise Resurrection. The scenes in the windows of King's College Chapel, Cambridge are a type/antitype scheme.

NEW TESTAMENT

The Passion Cycle
Entry into Jerusalem; Last Supper; Washing of the Disciples' feet; Agony in the Garden; Betrayal; Denial of Peter; Trial of Christ; Mocking of Christ; Flagellation; Crowning with Thorns; Ecce Homo; Stations of the Cross; Road to Calvary; Christ stripped of his Garments; Raising of the Cross; Crucifixion *(Virgin Mary and John or Virgin Mary and soldier, Longinus, with lance to Christ's right, John and Stephaton, with reed and sponge, to His left)*; Descent from the Cross; Pieta *(Virgin Mary supporting dead Christ)*; Joseph of Arimathea removing nails and taking Body for burial; Entombment; Resurrection; 3 Maries at the Tomb; Mary Magdalene encountering Christ at Tomb *(noli me tangere)*; Journey to Emmaus; Supper at Emmaus (with two disciples); Incredulity of Thomas; Ascension; Descent of the Holy Ghost.

The Stations of the Cross
Jesus condemned to death; Jesus receives the Cross; Jesus falls under the Cross; Jesus meets the Virgin Mary; Simon of Cyrene bears the Cross; Veronica wipes the face of Jesus; Jesus falls for the second time; Jesus meets the women of Jerusalem; Jesus falls for the third time; Jesus is stripped of His garments; Jesus is nailed to the Cross; Jesus dies on the Cross; Jesus is taken down from the Cross; The body of Jesus is laid in the sepulchre.

The Life of the Virgin
Joachim and Anne, *parents of the Virgin*; Nativity; Presentation; Marriage; Annunciation; Visitation; Death; Assumption; Coronation.
The Virgin also appears in other scenes:
Nativity; Adoration of the Shepherds; Adoration of the Magi; Circumcision of Christ; Presentation in the Temple *(prophecy of Simeon)*; Flight into Egypt; Dispute with the Doctors.

Miracles and Parables
Marriage at Cana *(changing water into wine)*; Feeding of the 4000 *(with 7 loaves and a few fishes)*; Feeding of the 5000 *(with 5 loaves and 2 fishes)*; Raising of Lazarus from the Dead; Miraculous Draught of Fishes; Sermon on the Mount *(The Beatitudes)*; Return of the Prodigal son; The Good Shepherd; The Good Samaritan; and so on.

OLD TESTAMENT
Creation; Adam and Eve; Noah and the Flood; Abraham and Isaac; Jacob and Esau; Jacob's Ladder; Joseph and the Coat of Many Colours; Moses; Joshua; Samson; Ruth; David; Solomon; Esther; Jonah and the Whale.

APOCRYPHA
Tobias and the Angel; Judith and Holofernes; Susanna and the Elders.

ATTRIBUTES & ALLEGORY

20

TEXTS

The same biblical texts were repeatedly used in inscriptions and wall paintings. Their usual sources are the St James Authorised Version of the Bible, the Latin bible, the Book of Common Prayer or the Roman Catholic Missal.

Ave Maria, Creed, Sanctus	Book of Common Prayer
The Beatitudes	Matthew, chap. V to VII
The Fruits of the Spirit	Paul's Letter to the Galatians, chap. V
The Gifts of the Holy Spirit	Isaiah, chap. XI
The Magnificat	Luke, chap. I, vv. 46 to 55
Words from the Cross	Luke, chap. XXIII, vv. 34,43,46; John, chap. XIX, vv. 26,28,30; Matthew, chap. XXVII, vv. 46

OLD TESTAMENT
Allegory

Altar of sacrifice or burnt offering	old testament worship
Apple	Fall of Man
Ark of the Covenant	presence of God
Bricks	captivity of Israel
Bullock and censer	Day of Atonement
Butterflies	escape of soul to afterlife
Caterpillars	man's earthly life
Distaff	destiny of Eve
Doorposts and lintel	God's protection at Passover
Dove with olive branch	peace and forgiveness
Dragon	Satan; sin; pestilence
Dragon (underfoot)	victory of good over evil
Flaming sword held by angel or Hand of God	expulsion of Adam from Eden
Grapes	entry into Canaan
Lamb (paschal lamb)	festival of passover
Lash	captivity of Israel
Lizards, beetles, snails	transience of life and decay of the body
Scroll	Torah or 5 books of Moses
Scroll with sheaf of wheat	Pentecost
Serpent	Satan
Serpent coiled around world	sinful nature of mankind
Serpent eating tail	serpent of eternity
Seven-branch candlestick (Menorah)	old testament worship
Spade	destiny of Adam

ATTRIBUTES & ALLEGORY
The Bible

Characters' attributes

Aaron	censer; flowering wand or rod in hand
Abel	crook; lamb
Abraham	knife; shield
Amos	crook
Cain	plough
Daniel	ram with four horns
David	harp; lion
Deborah	crown
Elijah	fiery chariot; wheel of chariot; ravens
Esau	bow and arrows
Ezekiel	closed gate
Gideon	pitcher concealing torch
Hosea	cast off mantle
Isaac	cross formed of bundles of wood
Isaiah	saw; book; scroll
Jacob and family	sun, moon and 12 stars
Jeremiah	large stone
Jonah	whale
Joseph	coat of many colours
Joshua	trumpet; sword
Melchisedek	loaf and chalice
Micah	temple on mountain
Moses	bullrush basket; burning bush; horns; tablets
Nahum	feet appearing from cloud above mountain
Noah	ark; oar; dove with olive branch
Ruth	ear of wheat
Samson	jawbone of ass; pillars; wrestling with lion; head in lap of Delilah
Seth	thread wound 3 times around thumb
Solomon	temple (model of)
Zephaniah	sword over Jerusalem

Magi

Caspar	old man with long beard
Melchior	middle aged man with short beard
Balthazar	negro

Early decorators of churches used a whole series of symbols which had specific meanings for worshippers and clergy. Symbols can be confusing and need to be read in the right context. An eagle, for example, apart from being an attribute of St John the Evangelist, can also signify magnanimity or the Resurrection or kingship.

HAND OF GOD (MANUS DEI)

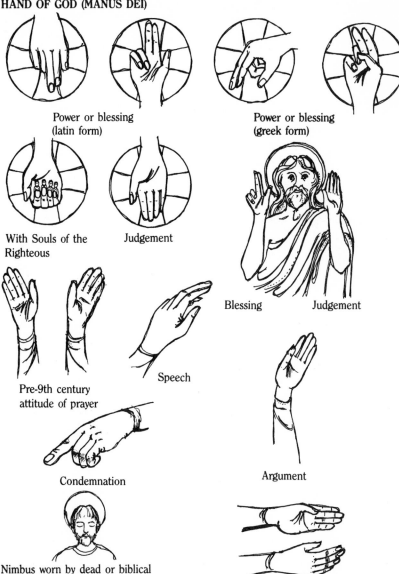

Power or blessing
(latin form)

Power or blessing
(greek form)

With Souls of the
Righteous

Judgement

Blessing   Judgement

Pre-9th century
attitude of prayer

Speech

Argument

Condemnation

Nimbus worn by dead or biblical
person *people living at the time of the
representation wear a square nimbus*

Supplication

23

ATTRIBUTES & ALLEGORY
Symbols

Stars

Seven Gifts of the Spirit

Nine Fruits of the Spirit

Twelve tribes of Israel

Regeneration

Creator

Epiphany

Sacred Monograms

Chi Rho
*the first 2 letters of the
Greek word for Christ*

IHC or IHS
*the first letters
of the Greek
spelling of Jesus*

Jesus Christ Victor
N = nika (victor)
or nostra (our)

Alpha and omega
*first and last letters
of the Greek alphabet
symbolising eternity*

Chi Rho with alpha
and omega within
a circle *Christ
for eternity*

Alpha mu omega
Christ within eternity
*yesterday, today
and evermore*

The cornerstone

SYMBOLS OF THE HOLY TRINITY

Trefoil

Triquetra

Bezel or
Interlocking triangles

Circle within triangle

Interwoven circles

Triquetra and circle

Holy Trinity

Trinity star
or Star of David

Equilateral triangle

The Three Fishes

The Three Hares

Triangle in circle

Three-rayed nimbus worn by
the Trinity

Shield with Doctrine
of the Blessed Trinity

ATTRIBUTES & ALLEGORY
Symbols
SYMBOLS OF THE PASSION CYCLE

 Crown of thorns

 Sponge on reed

 Nails

 Thirty pieces of silver

 Scourges

 Hammer and pincers

 Dice and seamless robe

 The cock that crowed

 Cross with sheet

 Pillar and cords

 The Title

 Fist

 Lantern

 Jug of vinegar

 Five wounds

 Agony in Gethsemane

 Ladder

 Sword and staff

GIFTS OF THE HOLY SPIRIT

Seven Lamps or Seven Flames

Seven Doves

The Holy Spirit
The Dove

Agnus Dei with
Book of Seven Souls

Agnus Dei with
Banner of Victory

The Pelican in her Piety
*the pelican piercing its breast to feed
its young with its blood is a symbol
of Christ's sacrifice on the cross.*

The Greek word for fish *signifies
Jesus Christ, son of God, Saviour*

Paschal Lamb

ATTRIBUTES & ALLEGORY
Symbols

SYMBOLS OF THE BLESSED VIRGIN MARY (BVM)

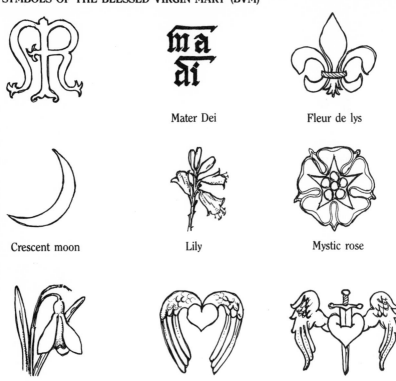

Mater Dei

Fleur de lys

Crescent moon

Lily

Mystic rose

Snowdrop

Winged heart

Pierced heart

SYMBOLS OF TEMPORAL POWER

Temporal figures may carry a staff of office or a specific symbol signifying power and authority. Archbishops, bishops and abbots may carry a crozier or pastoral staff. The pastoral staff will be carried in the right hand except during benediction when it will be in the left hand.

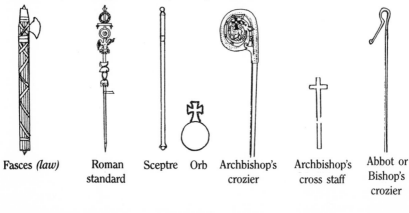

Fasces *(law)*

Roman standard

Sceptre Orb

Archbishop's crozier

Archbishop's cross staff

Abbot or Bishop's crozier

ATTRIBUTES & ALLEGORY
Symbols

GROUPS OF SEVEN
Seven is the symbolic number of perfection.

Gifts of the Holy Spirit
Counsel
Godliness
Holy Fear
Knowledge
Strength
Understanding
Wisdom

Liberal Arts
(sometimes accompanied by virtues)
Arithmetic
Astronomy
Geometry
Grammar
Logic
Music
Rhetoric

Sacraments
Baptism
Confirmation
Communion (Eucharist)
Penance (Confession)
Holy Orders
Matrimony
Extreme Unction

Vices or Deadly Sins
Anger
Covetousness
Envy
Gluttony
Lust
Pride
Sloth

Virtues	
Faith	holding cross; chalice; foot resting on square stone block
Hope	holding anchor; eyes and hands raised to Heaven; wings
Charity	nursing child; surrounded by children; holding flames; holding heart
Justice	scales; sword; blindfolded
Prudence	2 heads; holding mirror; holding snake; dragon
Temperance	pouring liquid from one vessel to another (watering the wine); sheathed sword; 2 vases
Fortitude	dressed in armour resembling Minerva; sword; club; shield; broken pillar; lion

COSTUME
Biblical

COSTUME

Costumed figures are encountered in stained glass scenes, in monuments and brasses and in paintings in churches. Some of these figures are drawn from imagination and some from life. The variety of costumes represented is great, but may give the key to date and period. The chapter on *COSTUME* covers a range of periods, but is inevitably oversimplified and only a small sample of the styles encountered.

Biblical

Biblical figures may be portrayed in mediaeval or contemporary costume. Authentic biblical dress was influenced by that of the many lands with which society came into contact.

Hebrew

Basic Hebrew costume was a long tunic with girdle, loose open cloak, sandals, nomad's headdress of square cloth bound with cord, or a pointed cap with or without a scarf wound around the base and the **tallith** *(a striped fringed prayer shawl)*. Women wore a long tunic covered by a shawl or long veil. An Israelite priest wore a **mitre** or a turban with an inscribed gold plate.

Egyptian, Persian and Byzantine

Men wore a loose fitting **robe**; Egyptian women wore a **kalasiris**, **sari** or **sheath**, though may be shown wearing a robe only. Egyptian men wore a **kilt** or **loin cloth**, sometimes with an **apron**. The blue and white striped linen head-covering with a cobra emblem attached to a gold fillet is a **khat** or **nemes**; the hat-like headgear is a **crown**. Assyrians wore a pot-shaped hat called a **mitre** and a king sometimes wore a **diadem** headband.

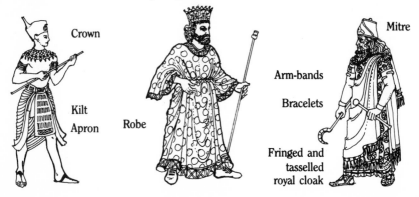

Crown

Kilt
Apron   Robe

Mitre

Arm-bands

Bracelets

Fringed and
tasselled
royal cloak

COSTUME

Roman Officer
with crested helmet

Military Cloak

Baldric from
left shoulder

Cuirass with
pendant strips

Tunica

Laced boots

Roman Legionary
Plain Helmet with
top knob

Leather Jacket

Metal Armour

Shield with
thunderbolt
device

Tunica

Leggings

Greek warriors wore
greaves and carried
circular shields

Sandals

Roman Patrician

Laurel Wreath

Tunic

Toga with borders
coloured according
to rank

Plebians wore a
tunic and cloak

Greek men wore a
long or short **chiton**
(tunic) and a large
himation or small
chlamys over it.
Scholars may have
omitted the chiton
and appear to be
wearing a toga.

Married Roman Lady

Greek women
wore the same
costume as
men, unless
they were
Amazons

Palla

Stola or
Dalmatic

COSTUME

COSTUME
English 9th to 12th Centuries

Phrygian cap

Knee length tunic with tight-fitting sleeves

Braies with crossbinding

Long or short veil

Super tunic pulled up into belt

Long cloak *(or circular cloak with head opening near one edge)*

Tunic

Short braies

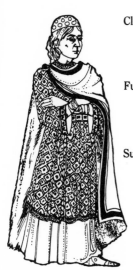

Close fitting cap

Fur-lined cloak

Super tunic

Tunic

Fillet or coronet over veil and wimple

Figure-fitting gown with lined hanging sleeves and corselet

Girdle wound twice round body

Mantle lined with fur or contrasting colour

English 13th and 14th Centuries

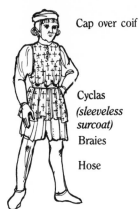

Cap over coif

Cyclas
(sleeveless surcoat)

Braies

Hose

Hood or chaperon

Cotehardie or surcoat worn over undertunic

Hood over a wimple

Gardcorp or gardecors

Fillet

Cloak with dagged edges

Gipon with low belt and buttoned sleeves

Hose

Coif or fillet worn over barbette and crispine

Loose surcoat

Kirtle

Widow's veil and wimple

Sideless cotehardie worn over kirtle

Widow or Avowess

Coif

Hood with Liripipe

Hat worn over hood

Chaplet

COSTUME
English 15th Century

Prayer beads
Purse
Dagger or
baselard

Chaperon and liripipe

Neckchain

Long gown (worn over
doublet and hose)

Heart shaped headdress with
veil above a fret or caul

Houpelande *(voluminous
circular gown with central hole
for head and sliced at sides to
form pointed hanging sleeves;
high waisted for women;
waisted for men)*

Kirtle

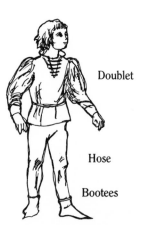

Jerkin with slit hanging
sleeves worn over doublet
and hose

Belt with
tongue

Doublet

Hose

Bootees

Pedimented headdress
with veil

Partlet

Low-necked gown

Heraldic Mantle fastened by
cords

Large belt with buckle and
attached ornaments

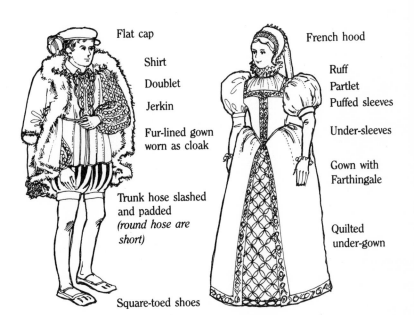

Flat cap

Shirt

Doublet

Jerkin

Fur-lined gown
worn as cloak

Trunk hose slashed
and padded
*(round hose are
short)*

Square-toed shoes

French hood

Ruff
Partlet
Puffed sleeves

Under-sleeves

Gown with
Farthingale

Quilted
under-gown

COSTUME

35

COSTUME
English 17th Century

Falling Band

Slashed sleeves

Padded doublet

Tassets on basque

Full Breeches

Wig

Cravat

Coif

Collar

Tippet

Lace Collar

Doublet

Knee breeches

Bucket topped boots

Gown

Tall hat with ribbon loops

Short doublet

Cloak

Breeches

Jabot

Coat

Tricorne

Close fitting breeches with roll top stockings

Pinner cap

Sack or saque-backed robe

Smock

Round-eared cap

Fichu

Chemise sleeves

Mob cap

Beaver hat

Chapeau-bras

Round hat

Queue

Skirt gathered upwards to reveal petticoat worn over hoop

37

COSTUME
English 19th Century

Epaulettes

Waistcoat

Knee-breeches
Stockings

Peg-top
trousers

Redingote with full skirts,
rolled collar and
shoulder cape

Sloping coat with white
facings

Double breasted
cut-away coat
and pantaloons

Tied cravat

Reticule

Frock coat

Pantalettes

38

Wimple with veil
13th century

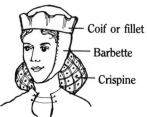

Coif or fillet
Barbette
Crispine

Crispine
13th/14th century

Goffered veil
14th century

Gorget
14th century

Heart shaped
15th century

Hood late
15th century

Reticulated
15th century

Butterfly
15th century

French Hood
16th century

Kennel or Gabled or
Pedimented
16th century

Hennin
15th century

Marie Stuart Cap
16th century

COSTUME

39

COSTUME
Military

Red cap
White undercap

Long beard and hair

White cloak with
Red Cross on
shoulder

Staff with metal
shield showing a
Red Cross on a
white ground

Knight Templar
13th century

Flat Helm

White surcoat
with red cross
on breast

Crusader
13th century

Morion helmet

Sleeveless jerkin

Doublet

Sash worn over
Cuirass

Swordbelt

Breeches

Musket

Hose

Thighboots

Soldier
c. 1590

Knights in armour are found on tombs and memorial brasses and individual pieces of armour may be depicted on all manner of decoration. Genuine armour and firearms were stored in churches and some may still be found over tombs, although often mixed up and put on the wrong tombs over the centuries. *(See MONUMENTS AND MEMORIALS: Brasses)*

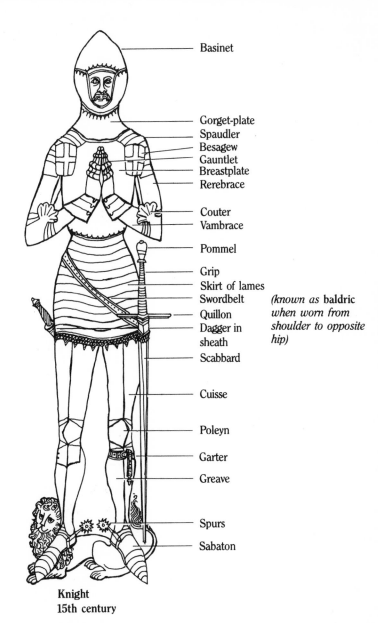

Basinet

Gorget-plate
Spaudler
Besagew
Gauntlet
Breastplate
Rerebrace

Couter
Vambrace

Pommel

Grip
Skirt of lames
Swordbelt   *(known as **baldric***
Quillon   *when worn from*
Dagger in   *shoulder to opposite*
sheath   *hip)*
Scabbard

Cuisse

Poleyn

Garter

Greave

Spurs

Sabaton

Knight
15th century

WEAPONS

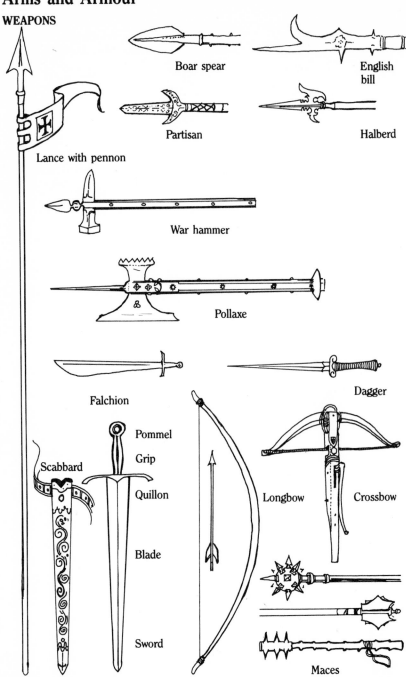

Boar spear

English bill

Lance with pennon

Partisan

Halberd

War hammer

Pollaxe

Falchion

Dagger

Scabbard

Pommel

Grip

Quillon

Blade

Sword

Longbow

Crossbow

Maces

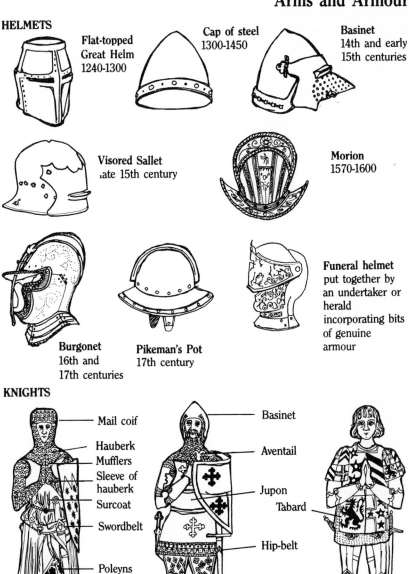

HELMETS

Flat-topped Great Helm 1240-1300

Cap of steel 1300-1450

Basinet 14th and early 15th centuries

Visored Sallet late 15th century

Morion 1570-1600

Burgonet 16th and 17th centuries

Pikeman's Pot 17th century

Funeral helmet put together by an undertaker or herald incorporating bits of genuine armour

KNIGHTS

Mail coif
Hauberk
Mufflers
Sleeve of hauberk
Surcoat
Swordbelt
Poleyns
Chausses

Early 14th century knight

Basinet
Aventail
Jupon
Tabard
Hip-belt

14th century knight

16th century knight

COSTUME

43

COSTUME
Vestments

Alb	full length belted white tunic with narrow sleeves. **Anglican version** possibly apparelled at neck and hem or trimmed with a lace flounce. **Catholic version** often embroidered.
Amice	white linen neck-cloth sometimes with an apparel at one edge.
Apparel	decorated panel applied to dalmatics, albs and amices.
Biretta	black, purple, red or white ridged hat, worn according to rank by priest, bishop, cardinal or pope.
Cassock	button through gown, coloured according to rank, or (monks) of appropriate colour of habit for order.
Chasuble	circular or oval cape with central head opening and **orphreys**; the principal vestment worn by an officiating priest. Full tent-like chasuble often known as **romanesque.**
Cope	semicircular cape fastened with a **morse**, decorated with a hood and orphreys. 20th century copes are often hand-worked in combinations of kid-leather, beads, jewels, metallic threads, cords and stitchery, incorporating a variety of symbols.
Dalmatic	sleeved open-sided tunic, worn by deacons, decorated with stripes called **clavi** and sometimes with apparels.
Girdle	white or coloured cord belt with tassels.
Hood	flat vestigal hood attached at back of mitre also worn by graduates in colours according to type of University degree.
Lappets	pair of ribbands attached at back of mitre.
Maniple	decorated band worn over the left arm, resembling a short stole, orginally a towel and purse combined.
Mitre	peaked headdress worn by bishops, pope and abbots: simplex = *white;* aurifrigiata = *gold or silver on white;* pretiosa = *jewelled.*
Morse	metal or embroidered clasp attached to broad band across chest, used to fasten cope.
Mozetta	short hooded cape, buttoned down front, coloured as biretta.
Orphrey	embroidered band, usually applied, found on chasubles and copes. On altar frontals, orphreys are decorative panels.
Pallium or Pall	originally a woollen vestment worn by archbishops, usually shown as a narrow Y-shaped strip with embroidered crosses, falling down the centre front and back.

Pastoral staff or Crozier stave carried by high dignitaries on which may be a cross, crook or horizontal crook (**Tau stave**); some times a **vexillium** *(scarf)* is attached.

Rochet similar to alb but shorter, either sleeveless or sleeves gathered at wrist.

Stole decorated band worn round the neck, beneath the chasuble, resembling, but longer than, the maniple; usually with a device at each end and a cross at the neck.

Surplice white gown, differing from the alb by long flowing sleeves, worn unbelted over the cassock.

Tiara headdress of pope.

Tunicle similar to dalmatic, although longer when worn by bishops with a dalmatic; it has narrow sleeves and no apparels except occasionally near the neck; it is usually worn by sub-deacons.

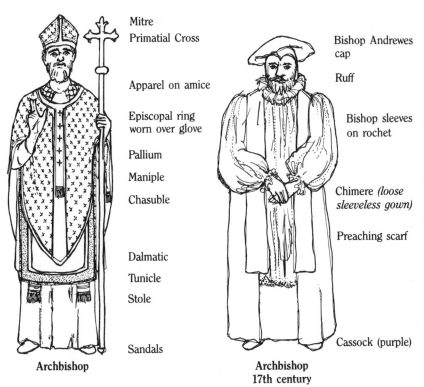

Mitre
Primatial Cross

Apparel on amice

Episcopal ring worn over glove

Pallium

Maniple

Chasuble

Dalmatic
Tunicle
Stole

Sandals

Archbishop

Bishop Andrewes cap

Ruff

Bishop sleeves on rochet

Chimere *(loose sleeveless gown)*

Preaching scarf

Cassock (purple)

Archbishop 17th century

COSTUME

COSTUME
Vestments

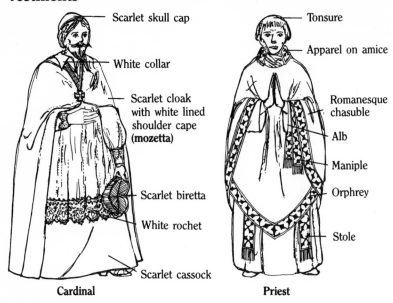

Scarlet skull cap

White collar

Scarlet cloak with white lined shoulder cape (**mozetta**)

Scarlet biretta

White rochet

Scarlet cassock

Cardinal

Tonsure

Apparel on amice

Romanesque chasuble

Alb

Maniple

Orphrey

Stole

Priest

DALMATICS

Dalmatic with clavi

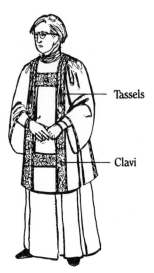

Tassels

Clavi

Dalmatic with tassels and clavi

ORPHREYS

Gothic
Y-shaped

V-shaped

Pallium-shaped

Gothic appliqued with
Chi-Rho, Alpha and
Omega motifs

Pillar shaped

COPES

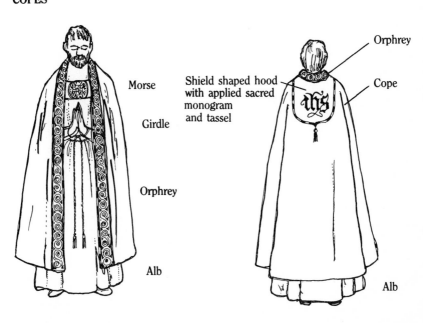

Morse

Girdle

Orphrey

Alb

Orphrey

Shield shaped hood
with applied sacred
monogram
and tassel

Cope

Alb

COSTUME

COSTUME
Vestments

Rounded fringed hood with hand-embroidered Maltese cross and orphreys of coloured velvet

Cowl hood

Lent/advent cope with embroidered Crown of Thorns, Eclipse of the Sun and Star of Advent motifs.

Organist's surplice

Preaching bands

Preaching stole   Deacon's stole

Preaching bands	(14 - 20 cm long)
Preaching stole	(127 cm long) worn uncrossed on surplice with small chain in front
Preaching scarves	usually gathered at neck with pinked ends (blue for readers; black for priests)
Vergers' gowns	divided sleeve and open front or closed front and velveteen trimmings
Organist's cassock	full skirt and semi-winged sleeves on surplice for ease of movement

Latin

Glory

Sovereignty

Calvary

Passion

Celtic

Iona

Cross and Thorny Crown

Saltire

Fimbriated

Adorned

Easter

Russian Orthodox

Lorraine

Patriarchal

Papal

St Peter's

St James's

Christus Rex

Crucifix

CROSSES

49

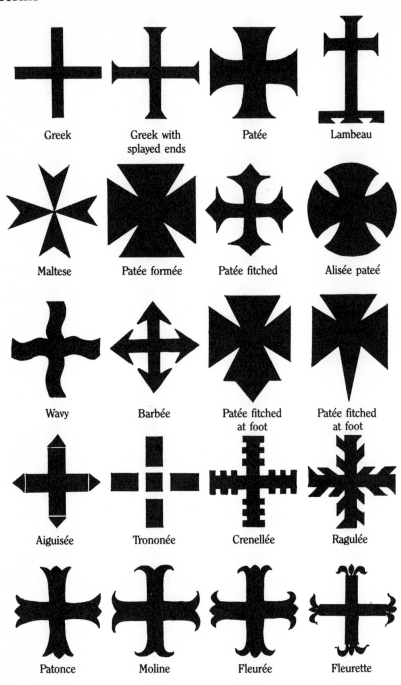

Greek

Greek with
splayed ends

Patée

Lambeau

Maltese

Patée formée

Patée fitched

Alisée pateé

Wavy

Barbée

Patée fitched
at foot

Patée fitched
at foot

Aiguisée

Trononée

Crenellée

Ragulée

Patonce

Moline

Fleurée

Fleurette

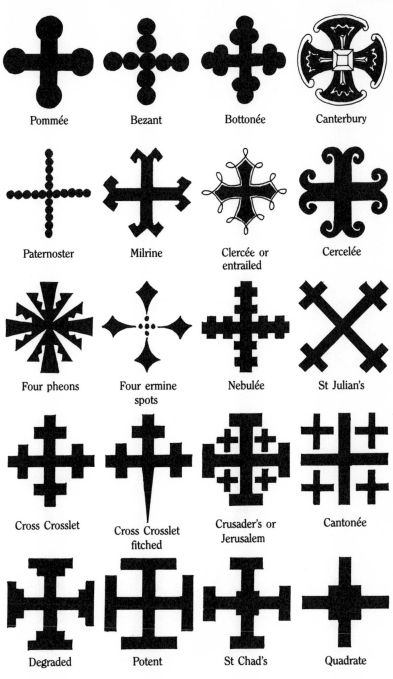

Pommée   Bezant   Bottonée   Canterbury

Paternoster   Milrine   Clercée or entrailed   Cercelée

Four pheons   Four ermine spots   Nebulée   St Julian's

Cross Crosslet   Cross Crosslet fitched   Crusader's or Jerusalem   Cantonée

Degraded   Potent   St Chad's   Quadrate

CROSSES

CROSSES
Terms

Parted and frettée   Triparted   Frettée   Masclée

Fylfot or Swastika   Potent rebated   Chain   Looped

Anchor   Alpha and Omega with Anchor cross   Y-shaped   Clavis

Latin cross fleurée   Tau   Ankh   Crux Ansata

Floriated quatrefoil   Circle and quatrefoil   Greek cross fleurée   Floriated octafoil

CROSSES

TERMS

Crucifix	cross with the image of Christ affixed
Crucifix of Christus Rex	crucifix with Christ figure in eucharistic vestments and crown
Christ in Agony	crucifix figure with open eyes
Corpus Christi or The Dead Christ	crucifix figure with closed eyes

Ivory Corpus Christi screwed onto oak Latin cross
Bearded head, with closed eyes, crowned with thorns, bowed to the right; arms upstretched; slightly curved torso with loose perizonium knotted over right hip; right knee bent; feet superimposed but nailed separately
Ivory scroll super-inscription attached with brass nail.

DECORATION
Friezes

Decorative friezes and motifs may appear on a variety of objects in a variety of materials as architectural mouldings, embroidery, painted decoration or carving.

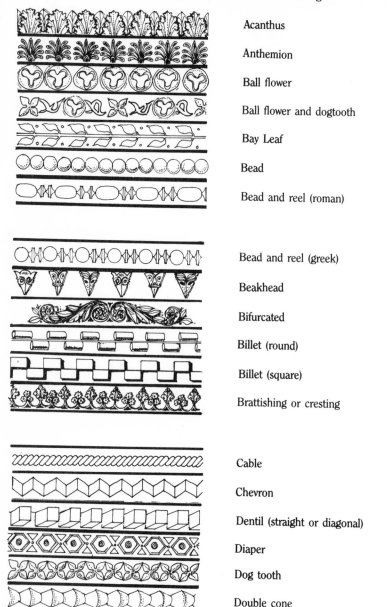

Acanthus

Anthemion

Ball flower

Ball flower and dogtooth

Bay Leaf

Bead

Bead and reel (roman)

Bead and reel (greek)

Beakhead

Bifurcated

Billet (round)

Billet (square)

Brattishing or cresting

Cable

Chevron

Dentil (straight or diagonal)

Diaper

Dog tooth

Double cone

Egg and tongue

Egg and dart

Embattled or battlemented

Enriched chevron

Festoon

Fleur-de-Lys

Four leaf flower

Fret or lattice or key or meander

Gadrooning, lobing or nulling

Gouging, channelling or adzed
(usually called scoop)

Guilloche

Husk

Imbricated interrupted by Tudor
ornament

Interlacing *(resembling strapwork and
moresque)*

Lotus alternating with palmette

Lozenge

Lunette

Meander

Moresque *(16th century term for
interlacing)*

Nailhead

Ovolo *(convex moulding)*

DECORATION
Friezes

Patera

Peardrop

Pellet

Plait

Reeding and fluting

Ribbon or ribband

Rosette *(rose patterned patera)*

Scalloped

Scratchwork and chipcarving

Scroll *(many variations)*

Shell

Strapwork

Swag

Tracery and blind or applied tracery

Trellis or lattice

Trilobed foliage

Tudor ornament

Tudor rose

Vine

Vitruvian scroll or running dog

Waterleaf

 Basketwork

 Grotesque

 Bucranium

 Mask

 Chinoiserie

 Medallions

 Cusping
*projecting point
where foils meet*

 Roundel

 Foils: trefoil,
quatrefoil, cinque-,
sex-, etc.

 Pendant

 Foliation

 Cherub, putto
or amorino

 Floriation

Flory and counter flory

DECORATION
Flora and Fauna

Fruits, flowers, trees and figures may have symbolic meaning *(see ATTRIBUTES & ALLEGORY)* or may simply serve a decorative purpose.

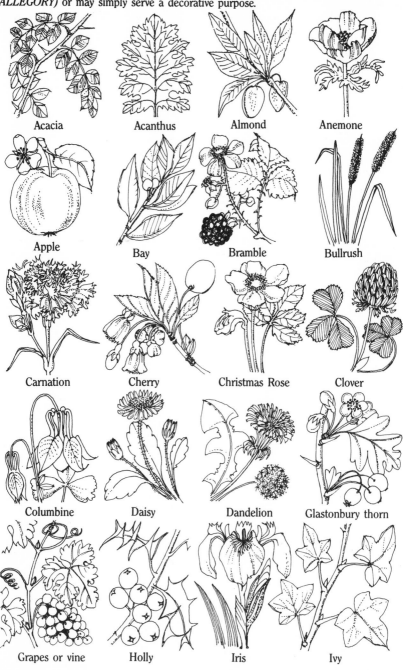

Acacia	Acanthus	Almond	Anemone
Apple	Bay	Bramble	Bullrush
Carnation	Cherry	Christmas Rose	Clover
Columbine	Daisy	Dandelion	Glastonbury thorn
Grapes or vine	Holly	Iris	Ivy

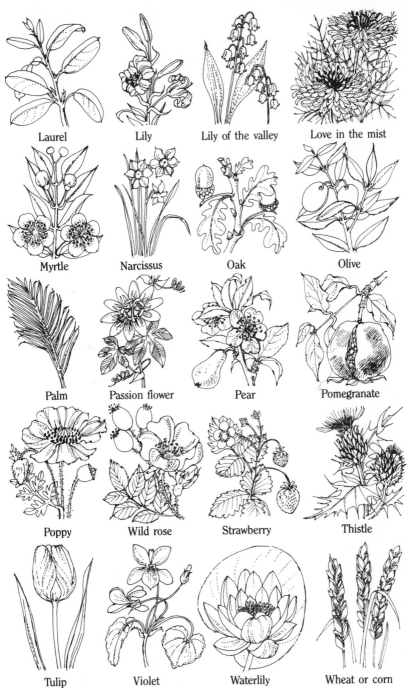

Laurel · Lily · Lily of the valley · Love in the mist

Myrtle · Narcissus · Oak · Olive

Palm · Passion flower · Pear · Pomegranate

Poppy · Wild rose · Strawberry · Thistle

Tulip · Violet · Waterlily · Wheat or corn

DECORATION
Flora and Fauna

Antelope, hind, hart, doe or stag

Basilisk or cockatrice

Centaur

Dragon

Wyvern

Griffin

Dolphin

Phoenix

Salamander

Unicorn

Wodehouse

Green man

Tree of Jesse
A branched tree with incorporated figures which combines the prophecy of Isaiah with the genealogical descent of Christ from Jesse (St. Matthew's Gospel, Chapter 1). The figures on the branches represent the Prophets, often in contemporary dress, and the kings of Judah in the line of David. The Virgin appears near the apex, holding the Child or with a figure of Christ above her and the Dove of the Holy Spirit.

Tree of Life   A naturalistic representation as a symbol of life, knowledge and salvation.

Tree of Life
Scroll frieze
14th century

DECORATION
Frames

Every edging, rim, border etc which encloses something is a frame. Frames are usually decorative and may be features in themselves. The same term is used for the skeleton of a piece of furniture.

Architectural frames	used for doors, windows, panels, tablets, medallions, niches, soffits, pictures, books etc.
Cartouche	frame in the shape of a scroll of parchment with turned up ends.
Frame	encloses a space with symmetrical decoration.
Partial frame	external ornament top and bottom to emphasise the vertical, the lower ornament having the general shape of a bracket and the upper making a cresting feature.
Strapwork frame	use of strapwork to surround or partially surround object; characteristic of Renaissance style, frequently with additional foliage and festoons. In books, strapwork often includes architectural forms.

Partial frame

Frame

Cartouche

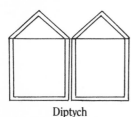

Strapwork frame

Strapwork bookplate

Diptych

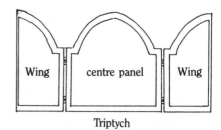

| Wing | centre panel | Wing |

Triptych

Painted mural decoration was common in pre-Reformation churches in Britain and constantly replaced and renewed. In the mid-16th century, many wall paintings were obliterated and some were overpainted with texts (**The Sentences**). In the 20th century some mediaeval paintings have been restored from beneath limewashing and overpainting. Subject matter was more important than artistic merit and few painters, except those working for royalty, are known.

Fresco	painting onto damp plaster usually employed in Italy but rarely in Britain
Secco	painting onto dry plaster, usually in red, yellow, white and black, commonly employed in Britain. Paintings applied by this method have a tendency to flake off the wall

Wall paintings should be read as a strip cartoon; they are sometimes in two or more tiers, the individual scenes being divided by architectural motifs or bordered top and bottom. Incidents are often telescoped so that figures at the end of one scene may be back to back with the figures in the next. Scenes are stylised. Good people have haloes; bad people are caricatured; accessories are enlarged out of proportion to emphasise rank, authority or cruelty. Costume is usually contemporary and will give a clue to the date of the work. Souls are usually naked figures but carry rank identifications *(see ATTRIBUTES & ALLEGORY)*.

Subjects group into 4 types:
Decorative masonry patterns 12th/14th centuries: scroll, chevron, heraldry, vine, diapering
14th/15th centuries: decoration characterised by clear stencilling
Bible stories including the Tree of Life and Tree of Jesse
Saints, apostles, martyrs and scenes from their lives
Moralities or allegorical themes containing warnings against particular sins including the Seven Deadly Sins, the Seven Works of Mercy, the Weighing of Souls and the Doom or Last Judgement.

The Doom
Christ, robed to display the Five Wounds, seated on a rainbow, judging the living and dead. He blesses with one hand and holds up an open palm of judgement with the other. His feet rest on a sphere. He is flanked by groups of the Heavenly Host, Apostles, Evangelists, the Virgin Mary and St John the Baptist. **Angels** bear the Symbols of the Passion or blow trumpets. **Scrolls** often bear *"Come ye blessed of my Father, and inherit your Kingdom"* on His right and *"Go ye evil doers into eternal fire"* on His left. Lower down, in the general resurrection St Peter receives the Blessed at the gate of Heaven and the sinners are damned in hellfire.

Alternation	two separate motifs repeated successively in the same order
Amphisbaena	devil facing both ways or double headed snake
Amphiscian	cockatrice with small dragon at end of tail
Arabesque	scrollwork, plant prints and flowing lines without figures
Asymmetry	unequal balance
Banderole	ribbon or scroll bearing inscription
Biomorphic	abstract motif based on natural forms
Chimera	monster usually with lion's head, goat's body and serpent's tail
Geometric	abstract motif based on lines and angles
Striate	lined
Symmetry	equal balance
Zoomorphic	of beastlike form

DECORATION
Wall Paintings

Rustication *any object or material that appears artificially weathered, particularly of incised blocks of stone.*

Trophy *decorative group of weapons, musical instruments or armour usually displayed with foliations, ribbons and flowers.*

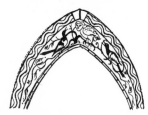

Owl and Magpie copied from a Bestiary illustrating *"idle chatterers mocking wisdom"* c. 1330

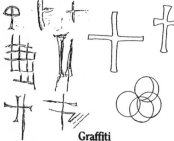

Graffiti
Mediaeval markings cut into stone or woodwork

Vertebrate band *continuous design, usually of flowers, fruit or foliage with the main stem running through the centre.*

Rinceau band *similar to vertebrate, but with a wavy central stem*

Allegorical vine border
13th century

Pelta or double axe pattern c. 1100

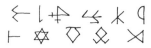

Mason's marks

Consecration crosses,
usually 12 within church (painted) and 12 without (carved)

Recording note: *Rubbings will give the best impression of incised wall marks. The size and location are important.*

A knowledge of the basic principles of heraldry will help in understanding monuments, stained glass windows, kneelers and embroidered banners.

Heraldic decoration can be described either by **blazoning** *(using correct heraldic terminology)* or **tricking** *(making a rough sketch with a detailed description of colours and motifs)* (see page 74). To identify a particular coat of arms it may help to look for another elsewhere in the church or graveyard under which there might be a helpful inscription. Church leaflets, the incumbent, local antiquarian societies and the local reference library will be helpful. It is impossible to trace every coat of arms, particularly those assumed illegally in Victorian times.

Women may display badges but are not entitled to display their arms on a shield nor are they permitted a helm or crest. They may display their arms in a lozenge or cartouche. The personal arms of a bishop are impaled with the arms of his see; an approach also applied to some officials.

Achievement	the complete armorial device, including shield, helm, crest, mantling, wreath, supporters, motto, etc. Usually referred to as **armorials** on plate
Badge	device denoting membership of a community, or strictly personal addition to coat of arms; worn by soldiers and servants of the mediaeval household
Base	bottom of shield
Chief	top of shield
Coat of Arms	displayed on the shield, lozenge or banner
Crest	device borne on the top of the helm
Crest Wreath	wreath hiding join between crest and helm
Dexter	left side as viewed from the front
Field	ground of shield
Hatchment	the armorial bearings of a deceased person, usually painted on canvas stretched across a lozenge-shaped frame, heavily painted to withstand the weather
Helm	helmet above shield, different according to rank
Insignia	a display of distinguishing marks of an office or honour
Mantling	drapery hanging from helm
Shield	central to heraldic device bearing arms; varied in shape but variance of no significance
Sinister	right side as viewed from the front

HERALDRY
Terms

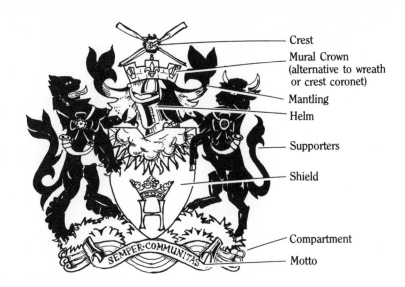

Crest

Mural Crown
(alternative to wreath
or crest coronet)

Mantling

Helm

Supporters

Shield

Compartment

Motto

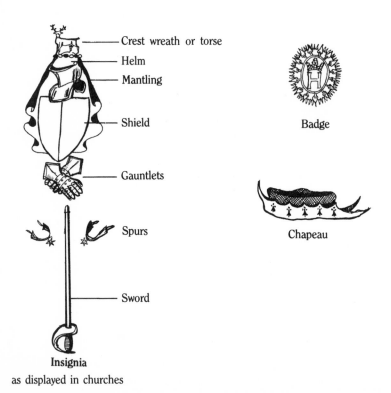

Crest wreath or torse

Helm

Mantling

Shield

Gauntlets

Spurs

Sword

Insignia
as displayed in churches

Badge

Chapeau

There is an exact terminology for armorial colours which will be indicated on records by the following markings. There are also certain rules. Except for the arms of Jerusalem, no metal is ever placed on metal, nor colour on colour, nor fur on fur.

METALS

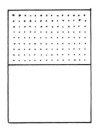

Gold: or

Silver: argent (arg.)

Black: sable (sa.)

Red: gules (gu.)

Blue: azure (az.)

Green: vert (vt.)

Purple: purpure (purp.)

Colours

Proper (ppr.) *denotes natural colours*

Furs

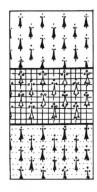

Ermine
arg. ermined sa.

Ermines
sa. ermined arg.

Erminois
or ermined sa.

Pean
sa. ermined or

Vair always arg. and az., *any colour variation produces* **vairy**

Potent

Roundels have a different terminology for tinctures.
Or= bezant;   Arg. = plate;   Gu. = torteau;   Az. = hurte;
Vt. = pomme;   Sa. = ogress or pellet

HERALDRY
Shields

DECORATION

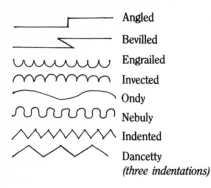

	Angled
	Bevilled
	Engrailed
	Invected
	Ondy
	Nebuly
	Indented
	Dancetty *(three indentations)*

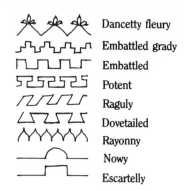

	Dancetty fleury
	Embattled grady
	Embattled
	Potent
	Raguly
	Dovetailed
	Rayonny
	Nowy
	Escartelly

SHIELDS

Chief

Dexter   Sinister

Base

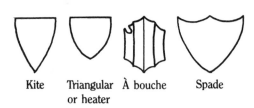

Kite   Triangular or heater   À bouche   Spade

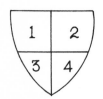

The numbering and precedence of a simple **quartered** shield,

Recording note: *Record the total number of quarterings together with the blazon at the tricking of the first quarter.*

Escutcheon of pretence, *indicates marriage to an heiress.*

The Red Hand of Ulster, *a distinguishing mark for baronets (except Nova Scotia)*

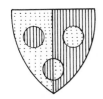

Per pale or and gu. three roundels counterchanged

Per pale

Per bend

Chequy

Per fess

Per bend sinister

Fusilly

Per saltire

Per chevron

Quarterly

Gyronny

A chief

Fretty

Gutty

Semy

HERALDRY
Creatures

CREATURES

Blackamoors	negroid, often with a serpent around the neck
Savages	white-skinned, bearded, naked and wreathed about the temple and loins
Saracens	white-skinned, bearded, clothed and wreathed about the temple

Lions

The terminology for describing posture may change according to the creature

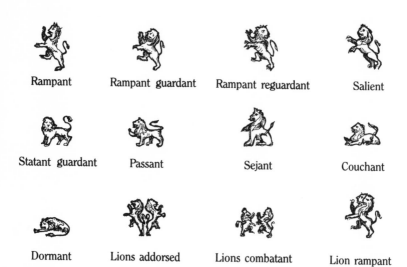

Rampant	Rampant guardant	Rampant reguardant	Salient
Statant guardant	Passant	Sejant	Couchant
Dormant	Lions addorsed	Lions combatant	Lion rampant double-headed

CADENCY MARKS denote seniority in a family and sometimes distinguish one branch from another

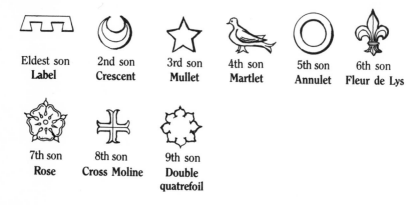

Eldest son	2nd son	3rd son	4th son	5th son	6th son
Label	**Crescent**	**Mullet**	**Martlet**	**Annulet**	**Fleur de Lys**

7th son	8th son	9th son
Rose	**Cross Moline**	**Double quatrefoil**

CROWNS AND CORONETS

Duke's coronet
8 strawberry leaves of equal height, 5 visible

Royal crown
worn by King and King's heir 4 crosses patée alternating with fleurs de lys

King's crown has diadems springing from the crosses and the junction is surmounted by a mount bearing another cross patée

Heir's crown is similar but with only two diadems

Marquess's coronet
4 strawberry leaves alternating with 4 pearls of equal height, 3 leaves and 2 pearls visible

Earl's coronet
8 pearls on long points alternating with 8 short strawberry leaves, 5 pearls and 4 leaves visible

Royal coronet worn by younger sons and brothers of kings similar to royal crown but without diadems and cross, surmounted by golden tassel

Viscount's coronet
16 pearls on rim, 8 or 9 pearls visible

Baron's coronet
6 pearls on rim, 4 visible

HELMS

King and royal family
gold, six bars affrontée

Earl, peer or baron
silver, garnished with gold,
four or five bars,
shown in profile

Baronet or knight
steel, vizor raised, affrontée

Gentleman or esquire
steel, vizor closed,
shown in profile

The heraldry of hatchments is not always accurate and the motto not always that of the family; silver and gold are indicated by white and yellow. The dexter side is the male side, except for bishops and others holding certain public office. The background is always black behind the arms of the deceased. Variations occur when the arms of more than one wife are depicted.

Married man deceased with surviving wife his arms on dexter black background impaling hers on sinister

Married woman deceased with surviving husband his arms on dexter white background impaling hers on black, sinister

Bachelor one shield on all black background

Bishop arms of see on dexter his own on sinister on black background; mitre and pastoral staves replace helm and crest

Spinster one coat of arms on lozenge on all black background without helmet or crest but sometimes including a cherub or ribbon bow

Wife of bishop Dexter shield of see impaling bishop; sinister on black background of bishop impaling wife

Widower his arms on dexter impaling her arms on sinister on black background (other wives, dead and living may be included)

Widow arms on lozenge, late husband's on dexter impaling hers on sinister on black background, crest, helm and motto omitted or replaced by ribbon knot

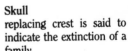

Skull replacing crest is said to indicate the extinction of a family

HERALDRY
Hatchments

TRICKING

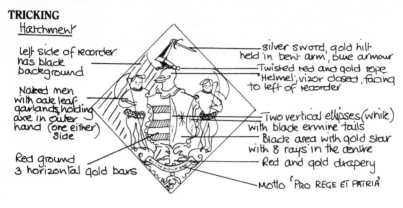

Hatchment

Left side of recorder has black background

Naked men with oak leaf garlands, holding axe in outer hand (one either) side

Red ground 3 horizontal gold bars

silver sword, gold hilt held in bent arm, blue armour

Twisted red and gold rope

Helmet; vizor closed, facing to left of recorder

Two vertical ellipses (white) with black ermine tails

Black area with gold star with 8 rays in the centre

Red and gold drapery

Motto 'PRO REGE ET PATRIA'

HATCHMENT OF DONALD CAMERON OF LOCHIEL d. 1858

BLAZONING

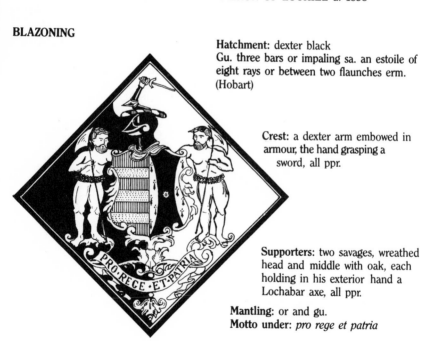

Hatchment: dexter black
Gu. three bars or impaling sa. an estoile of eight rays or between two flaunches erm. (Hobart)

Crest: a dexter arm embowed in armour, the hand grasping a sword, all ppr.

Supporters: two savages, wreathed head and middle with oak, each holding in his exterior hand a Lochabar axe, all ppr.

Mantling: or and gu.
Motto under: *pro rege et patria*

pre-1340
gules, three lions
passant guardant
in pale or

1340-1405
1 & 4 France
2 & 3 England

1405-1603
1 & 4 France modern
2 & 3 England

1603 - 1707
1 & 4 quarterly France
and England
2 Scotland
or, a lion rampant
within a double
tressure flory
counterflory gu.
3 Ireland
az., a harp or,
stringed arg.

1689-1702
1 & 4 quarterly
France and England
2 Scotland
3 Ireland
Escutcheon: arms of
Nassau
az. billetty
charged with
a lion rampant or

1707-1714
1 & 4 England impaling
Scotland
2 France modern
3 Ireland

1714-1801
1 England impaling
Scotland
2 France modern
3 Ireland
4 Hanover

1801-1816
1 & 4 England
2 Scotland
3 Ireland
Escutcheon: arms of
Hanover adorned with
bonnet

1816-37
1 & 4 England
2 Scotland
3 Ireland
Escutcheon: arms of
Hanover adorned with
crown

1837 onwards

Arms

quarterly, 1st and 4th (England), gu. three lions pass. guard. in pale or; 2nd (Scotland) or, a lion ramp. within a double tressure flory counterflory gu.; 3rd (Ireland) az. a harp or, stringed arg.; the whole encircled with the Garter

Crest	Upon the royal helmet, the imperial crown ppr., thereon statant guardant or, a lion imperially crowned also ppr.
Supporters	Dexter, a lion ramp. guard., or, crowned as the crest; sinister, an unicorn arg. armed, crined and unguled or, gorged with a coronet composed of crosses patée and fleurs de lys, a chain affixed thereto, passing between the fore-legs and reflexed over the back of last
Motto	*Dieu et mon Droit* in the compartment below the shield; with the Union rose, shamrock and thistle engrafted on the same stem
Crown of England	a circle or, issuing therefrom 4 crosses patée and 4 fleurs de lys, arranged alternately; from the crosses patée arise two arched diadems or ornamented with pearls, closing at the top under a mound, surmounted by a cross patée also or, the whole enriched with precious stones; cap of crimson velvet turned up erm.

Badges

England	red and white rose united
Scotland	thistle
Ireland	a harp or, string arg. Ireland shamrock leaf vt.
Wales	dragon pass. wings elevated gu. upon a mound vt.

All ensigned with the royal crown.

Recording Note: *A standard description "Royal Arms as used from 1837" can be used to replace full blazoning.*

Orders of Knighthood

The symbols of orders will appear on the insignia and the arms will include the motto.

The Order of the Garter buckle
"Honi soit qui mal y pense"
The Order of the Thistle saltire cross and thistle
"Nemo me impune lacessit"
The Order of St Patrick shamrock
"Quis separabit"
The Order of the Bath Maltese cross with rose, thistle and shamrock in centre
"Tria juncta in uno"
The Star of India
"Heaven's light our guide"
The Order of St Michael and St George
"Auspicium Melioris Aevi"
The Order of Victoria and Albert
Queen Victoria and Prince Albert in profile

ECCLESIASTICAL ARMS

Each see has its own arms. The chief provinces of the Church of England are the Archiepiscopal sees of Canterbury and York

Canterbury
az. an archiepiscopal cross in pale or surmounted by a pall ppr. charged with four crosses patée fitchée sa.

York
gu. two keys in saltire arg. in chief a regal crown

LETTERING
Terms

Lettering appears on memorials, in books and manuscripts, on stained and engraved glass and textiles. It is possible to consider a general approach to the classification of lettering but in addition, specific systems exist for the identification of silver, pewter and ceramics.

TERMS

Applied	individual letters cast or carved and pinned to the surface of buildings and memorials; commonly of gilded wood, brass, bronze and lead
Flat	painted directly onto the surface; a fine outline may show around letters painted on stone
Incised	cut into the surface. Letters may be painted in a colour or filled with lead or mastic

V-Cut	Gouged	Lowered	Cushioned

Raised   background cut away leaving letters in relief; may be raised, domed or raised with inline

Raised	Domed	Raised with inline

On manuscripts and in calligraphy, the capital and small letters are described as **majuscules** and **minuscules** respectively. However, printing has provided the widest terminology for describing letterforms. The terms **upper case** and **lower case** derive from the type cases of printers where the case of capital letters lies above that of small letters. Today, **capital letters** and **lower case letters** are the terms most generally understood when describing all lettering other than manuscripts.

Cap. line —
 x height —
 Base line —
 Drop line —

Serifs   Ascender   Descender

Weight   described as **light; medium; bold** or **extra bold**

Light	Medium	Bold	Extra bold

Width	described as **condensed** or **expanded**
	Latin condensed type or *Latin expanded type*

DISPLAYWORK **STAR**

Condensed	Expanded

Decorated letters	elaborations of a basic form
	Fry's ornamented type
Flourished	part of the basic letter, either roman or italic extended into a flourished shape.
	Perpetua type, italic capitals

REPRO *ADM*

Decorated	Flourished

Outlined/shaded	outlined or shaded to give the impression of a third dimension.
	Grotesque outline type or chisel shaded type

ABCD ABCab

Classical roman	the word **roman** has several meanings and it is important to distinguish between them. During the 1st century AD inscriptional lettering in Rome had its greatest flowering. The Trajan inscription is a fine example.

MP·CAES

Roman	printing term denoting both capital and lower case letters which are upright as opposed to sloped or italic and which have their roots in the classical roman letters
	Perpetua type, designed by Eric Gill

ABCEMORS
abcdefghimop

LETTERING
Types

Italic	sloped version of roman. The name stems from the letterforms of Italian writing masters of the 16th century which in fact hardly sloped at all.
Sloped roman	term used by letter designers, but italic is generally understood to refer to that style of letter which leans to the right
Perpetua italic type

ABCEMORST
abcdefghimnop

Sans serif	letterforms characterised by a lack of serifs and a more even width of stroke throughout each letter. Within this group are types variously described as **grotesque**, **glyptic** and, confusingly, **gothic** but sans serif is the simplest and most commonly used description.

ABC abcd ⌐

Clarendon	letters with bracketed serifs, derived from the typeface of that name. It is found incised on many 18th and 19th century gravestones.

ABCabcd

Egyptian	letters with square serifs, used extensively on memorials in various weights and sets. *Rockwell type*

ABC abcd

Latin	letters with triangular serifs.
Latin expanded type

ABCDEF
abcdefgh

Gothic letters with strong vertical pen stress, evenly spaced elements and angular terminals with wide variations showing condensation, expansion, decoration and flourishing. Also known as **black letter** in mediaeval manuscripts. *Old English type*

𝔄 𝔅 ℭ 𝔞𝔟𝔠

Copper plate well known 18th century pen style, preferable term to **italic** or **script**. *Marina script type*

Effect may be copied

MANUSCRIPT LETTERFORMS

Of the great variety of manuscript styles developed in Europe from the 1st century AD, these examples represent clear stages in the development of writing.

Majuscules Quadrata or *square capitals* from a 3rd century Virgil in the Vatican Library, Cod. Vat. 3256

RATESETMYSTICAVANN
AFAIVLIOANIEMEMORI

Rustica or *rustic capitals* from a 4th century Virgil in the Vatican Library, cod. Palat. Lat. 1631

TESTATVAMORITVRADEOS
SIDERATVMSIQVODNONA

Uncials from 5th century manuscript in the British Library, Cotton MS Vespasian A.i.

fecerunt ocul,

Half uncials from 7th century Lindisfarne Gospels, British Library, Cotton MS Nero D.iv.

abate bibere

LETTERING
Types

Versals   based on a 7th century manuscript

R A L O M

Roman   script based on 9th century Carolingian pen writing, Bodelian MS, E.D. Clarke 28

hunc ab ordo mo

Gothic   gothic book hand from 13th century York Psalter, British Library 54179

aboram clamant

Italic   Early 16th century italic script arrighi (attributed), British Library, Royal MS 12C VIII.

delectatio afferretur

TWO-DIMENSIONAL SHAPES

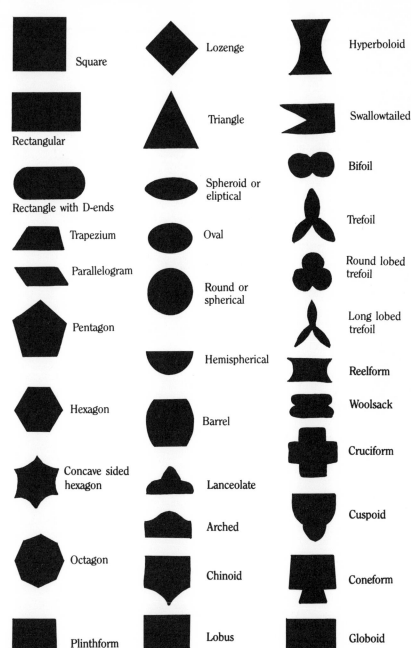

Square

Rectangular

Rectangle with D-ends

Trapezium

Parallelogram

Pentagon

Hexagon

Concave sided hexagon

Octagon

Plinthform

Lozenge

Triangle

Spheroid or eliptical

Oval

Round or spherical

Hemispherical

Barrel

Lanceolate

Arched

Chinoid

Lobus

Hyperboloid

Swallowtailed

Bifoil

Trefoil

Round lobed trefoil

Long lobed trefoil

Reelform

Woolsack

Cruciform

Cuspoid

Coneform

Globoid

SHAPES & MOULDINGS
Universal shapes
THREE-DIMENSIONAL SHAPES

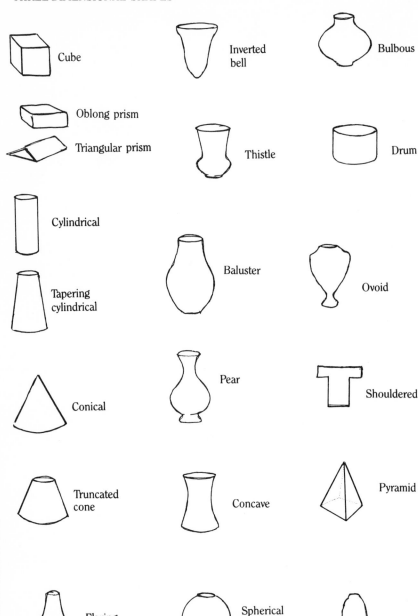

Cube

Inverted bell

Bulbous

Oblong prism

Triangular prism

Thistle

Drum

Cylindrical

Baluster

Ovoid

Tapering cylindrical

Conical

Pear

Shouldered

Truncated cone

Concave

Pyramid

Flaring

Spherical or convex

Bell

COMPLEX SHAPES

 Cusped

 Arched

 Trefoil head

 Cinquefoil head

 Ogee arched

 Ogival compartment

 Silesian or shouldered stem

 Bifurcated

 Splayed

 Fishtail

 Fleur-de-lys

 Lobed

 Segment

 Shell

 Cup and cover

 Volute

SHAPES & MOULDINGS
Cups, Plates and Jugs

Baluster
(or pear or tulip)

Baluster

Squat baluster

Bombe

Cylindrical

Tapering
cylindrical

Tall cylindrical

Tall tapering
cylindrical

Barrel

Barrel

Boat

Drum

Helmet

Urn (or vase
or ovoid)

Hexagonal.
stepped stand
or socle

Plate-shaped

Dish-shaped or
basin-shaped

Bowl-shaped or
saucer-shaped

Cup-shaped

SHAPES & MOULDINGS
Covers and Finials

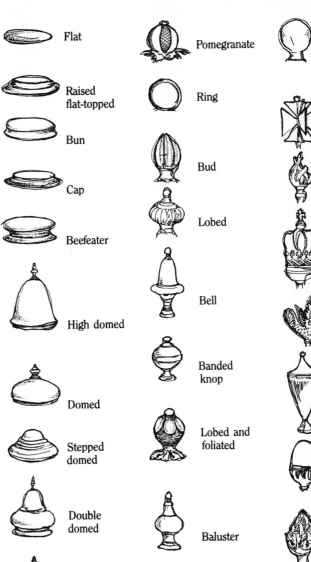

Flat

Raised
flat-topped

Bun

Cap

Beefeater

High domed

Domed

Stepped
domed

Double
domed

Waisted

Pomegranate

Ring

Bud

Lobed

Bell

Banded
knop

Lobed and
foliated

Baluster

Orb

Ball

Cross

Flame

Crown

Dove

Urn

Acorn

Cone

Ball and
steeple

SHAPES & MOULDINGS
Feet and Handles

 Arcaded

 Domed on narrow flange

 Stud

 Incurving

 Spreading skirt

 Standard or loop

 Lobed quatrefoil

 Shallow dome or spreading conical

 Angular

 Shaped lobed or wavy

 High conical

 Paw

 Tuck-in base on spreading rim

 Baluster

 Cusped tripod

 Bun

 Capped scroll

 Stepped circular

 Ball

 High circular

 Reeded base

 Scroll

 Trumpet

 Hexagonal spreading moulded

 Broken or double scroll

 Circular moulded spreading

 Shell and scroll

 Flying scroll

SHAPES & MOULDINGS

88

Spherical

Compressed
or proper

Lobed

Wrythen
or spiralling

Hexagonal

Lobed gothic

Wrythen gothic

Compressed
and annulated

Bladed
(or flange)

Compressed
knot above
a flange

Lobed flange

Swelling

Cup and cover
or melon

Shouldered

Mushroom

Dumb-bell

Cushioned

Cone

Acorn

Multi-knotted

SHAPES & MOULDINGS
Mouldings

Mouldings are plain or enriched projecting or recessed bands of decoration either worked directly (struck) or applied.

Bead and butt   moulding worked on 2 sides of panel
Bead and flush   moulding worked on all 4 sides of panel
Pulvinated   with cushion-like swelling
Quirk   groove running parallel to bead

The names of mouldings follow classical rules for all styles except gothic mouldings which have their own terminology, here represented in brackets where the moulding style exists.

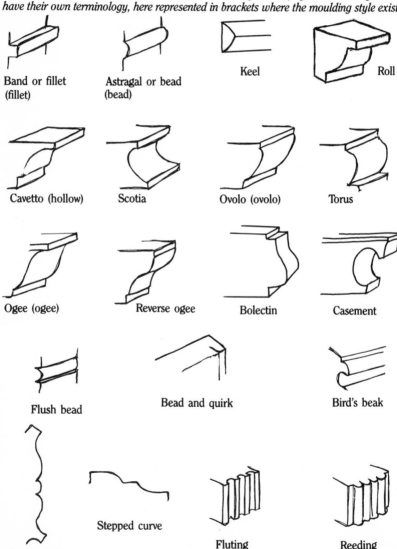

Band or fillet (fillet)

Astragal or bead (bead)

Keel

Roll

Cavetto (hollow)

Scotia

Ovolo (ovolo)

Torus

Ogee (ogee)

Reverse ogee

Bolectin

Casement

Flush bead

Bead and quirk

Bird's beak

Toad back

Stepped curve

Fluting

Reeding

MATERIALS

CERAMICS
Marks

Ceramics include objects made of porcelain, pottery and glass. Ceramics are occasionally encountered in churches, possibly a piece of mediaeval pottery appropriated by a flower arranger or a container of value that has been lent or donated, even a cracked mid 18th century piece which may have become a desirable collector's item.

Ceramics are not common in churches and if you do find a piece you will probably need a detailed reference book. *See FURTHER READING.*

PORCELAIN   is *translucent* unless the body is very thick. The body is white and almost invariably has a transparent glaze, which may be slightly blued. Vases are glazed inside and out, as glazing is part of the basic firing process.

POTTERY   is *opaque*, the clay body varying from brown, grey, red, orange to white. When the body is not white, a white opaque glaze may be used to imitate porcelain. Pottery is porous so has to be glazed, at least on the inside, if it is to hold liquid.

MARKS

Many ceramic pieces will be marked with the sign of origin, applied usually on the base, in either underglaze blue or impressed, incised or painted over the glaze. Factory trade marks can be forgeries or legitimate imitations. The Worcester factory, for example, not only used their own mark, but also the personal marks of their master-potters, oriental marks and even those of Meissen, Sevres, Tournay, Chantilly and others. "Flight", "Barr" and "Chamberlain" are names used by Worcester between 1783 and c.1840.

Between 1842 and 1883 a registration mark was used by many factories to protect a design from copying by rivals, the marks changing. An item marked *"England"* dates from 1891 an item marked *"Made in England"* dates from the 20th century.

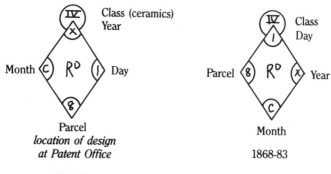

Class (ceramics)
Year
Month
Day
Parcel
location of design at Patent Office

1842-67

Class
Day
Parcel
Year
Month

1868-83

simple number only
1884-1901

An enormous variety of different wares may be found in churches. References are given only to the most common.

Meissen but copied and adapted by numerous factories.

Bow, Chelsea, Derby, Venice, or 19th century copies all used an anchor mark but the shape may vary.

Derby c. 1785-1830 similar marks in red, blue or purple, or incised

18th century English soft paste.

typical fancy outline used by Victorian factories, usually incorporating the pattern name and number

Wedgwood
note the full mark, lettering and spelling, as other firms using the name, often spelt **Wedgewood**, would not be genuine.

18th century **Sparrow Beak** jug, small with ribbed, smooth or patterned surfaces.

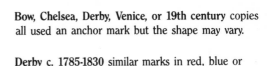

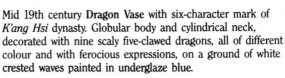

Mid 19th century **Dragon Vase** with six-character mark of *K'ang Hsi* dynasty. Globular body and cylindrical neck, decorated with nine scaly five-clawed dragons, all of different colour and with ferocious expressions, on a ground of white crested waves painted in underglaze blue.

Recording Note: *Record the mark accurately and in detail with a photograph or drawing and a note of the shape, glaze, colour and design. Recognise the difference between under glazed and overglazed decoration. Record even unmarked underglazed items. Anything handpainted, unless obviously of amateur workmanship, is of interest.*

CERAMICS
Floor Tiles

MEDIEVAL FLOOR TILES

PLAIN TILES

Used from about 1150, plain tiles were usually made by itinerant monks from local clays, often fired on site. These tiles are usually about 3-4 cm thick and about 10 cm square. Colours vary according to the clays used but are usually in the red-brown range. The tiles were originally glazed using raw lead ore which usually fired to a honey or greenish shade owing to the impurities it contained. Sometimes the raw tile was dipped in white slip (or liquid) clay before glazing and firing and this produced buff to greenish tiles which were often laid chequerwise with the red-brown tiles. This type of flooring has continued virtually unaltered up to fairly modern times.

MOSAIC TILES

From about 1180, tiles began to be cut into intricate shapes, often interlocking, which were usually laid to form large roundels, sometimes set in between square panels of mosaic or square tiling. Slip coated tiles were again used to add colour to the designs, which were often Moorish in influence and occasionally impressed or encaustic tiles were used *(see below)*.

IMPRESSED TILES

Early impressed tiles, c. 1200, were made by carving a simple geometric design onto a block of wood which was then hammered onto the surface of the tile to produce an intaglio pattern. From about 1250, designs became more complex and varying depths of relief were used to obtain different effects. Square tiles were sometimes impressed with a line design to simulate the earlier mosaic tiles and impressed details were occasionally used for added effect on encaustic tiles (such as the eye on a lion design).

ENCAUSTIC TILES

These tiles first appear about 1180-1200 and were formed by impressing the surface of the unfired tile with a wooden block and then filling the resulting depressions with white slip (liquid) clay. This produced a white design in the red body which when fired became buff in brown. Although usually about 10-12 cm square and 3 cm thick, these tiles were made in many varied shapes and sizes and were, on occasion, used as wall tiles. These tiles gradually became the standard type of mediaeval church tile, although some impressed tiles were still produced. Encaustic tile manufacture gradually became more localised and several clear manufacturing centres emerged, the most prolific being that at Tylers Green, Penn, Buckinghamshire. Later tiles from Penn are thought to have been made by a form of printing where the wood stamp was dipped in the slip and then hammered onto the top of the unfired tile, which was scraped level, glazed and fired. These "printed" tiles tend to look quite primitive but were an attempt at mass production to meet the growing demand during the 15th century. The art of encaustic tiling died out with the dissolution of the monastries and did not reappear until Victorian times.

Fleur-de-lys between four quadrants, each enclosing an embattled quadrant and a quarter octofoil. (Penn)

Design based on the Solomon's Seal with a quatrefoil at the centre within a star. (Penn)

Part of a four-tile design of formal foliage in a quatrefoil, with foliage and fleurs-de-lys cut out by a quadrant in the outer angles. Parts of the ground have fallen away. (Wessex)

Part of a continuous pattern of cinquefoils within circles powdered with lozenges, set in a square with foliated motifs in the spandrels and centre, alternating with squares enclosing fleurs-de-lys back to back. (Wessex)

CERAMICS
Floor Tiles

VICTORIAN FLOOR TILES

QUARRY TILES

Although this term is often applied to a wide range of plain floor tiles it is correctly used only for tiles which are moulded, cut or extruded from plastic (or wet) clay and unglazed. These tiles were much used in Victorian times for the aisles of churches and were usually laid in chequer pattern using red and black or red and buff tiles. The most common size is 15 cm square but 10 cm and 22.5 cm were also used. Mainly produced in the Potteries and Wales these tiles often have a coarse surface which contrasts with the smooth flat surface of dustpressed tiles.

DUSTPRESSED TILES

In 1840, Richard Prosser of Birmingham patented a method of producing ceramic buttons by drying clay to a fine dust which was then put in a powerful press, thus forming the button rapidly and accurately. Herbert Minton bought a share in the patent and realized that the process could be applied to the manufacture of tiles and by 1842 was producing smooth flat floor tiles in several colours. Because they were easier to clean than quarry tiles they soon became very popular and were used in the same way as quarry tiles or to form surrounds for encaustic tiles *(see below)*. As well as squares, many other shapes were made which were usually based on geometric portions of a 15cm square and these were laid utilising the many colours in large mosaic designs known as **Geometric Pavements**.

ENCAUSTIC TILES

Herbert Minton produced reproductions of mediaeval encaustic tiles for use in "Gothic revival" restorations from about 1835. Victorian encaustic tiles are easily recognized as they are usually far more precise and mechanical in design and manufacture than their predecessors. By 1860 many new colours had been introduced, often as many as eight on a single tile. Early tiles are normally unglazed or glazed over the inlay only, using a yellow majolica glaze. Later tiles, from about 1850 onwards, usually have a clear glaze or are fired to a higher (vitreous) temperature which makes them much less porous. Victorian encaustic tiles are quite often marked with the makers' name on the back and sometimes a "trade" tile was included which gives the makers' name and address, common makers' names are Mintons, Maws, Godwins, Craven Dunnill and Campbells.

Four fold foliate design in quartrefoil. Block printed in black on white body under clear glaze. Manufactured by MINTON HOLLINS & CO (Minton & Co) c. 1845. Prossers Patent Dustpressed Method. (Marks moulded on reverse)

Sacred Monogram IHS interlaced in provincal shaped cartouche with quarter roses at corners. Red White, Yellow Orange Mauve & Blue "Majolica" Glazes on dust pressed body. MINTONS & CO c. 1855 (Marks moulded on reverse)

Encaustic tile with design of St George on horseback based on a medieval original from the Temple Church, London. Design adapted by A.W.N. Pugin for Herbert Minton. c. 1850 (MINTON & CO. impressed on reverse) Unglazed.

Pseudo Medieval Encaustic tile with cinquefoil in wheel and stylized foliate corners. Surface "distressed" to represent medieval tile. W. GODWIN c. 1865 (Impressed marks on reverse) Worn glaze.

METAL
Terms

There are metal objects all around churches, some are precious, some workaday; some are functional, some merely decorative; some have much in common with ceramics, some with wooden objects, some with stone.

Various aspects of metal objects are of interest, their use, the metal they are made of, the marks, armorials and inscriptions they bear, their size and date. Decoration, particularly in mediaeval work, often demonstrates the same features and style as contemporary architecture.

TYPES OF METAL

Bell metal	grey-tinged alloy of copper and tin
Brass	alloy of copper and zinc
Britannia metal	similar to silver or polished pewter but in different designs to pewter; in use from 1790 to the 19th century
Bronze	alloy of copper, tin and other metal
Electroplate	method of silver plating introduced in 1840's; metallic appearance with straight seams
EPBM	electroplated Britannia metal (after 1850) with one vertical seam. Parts may be pewter and copper base may show at seam. Makers' names and catalogue numbers impressed into metal.
EPGS	electroplated German silver (electroplated nickel silver)
EPNS	electroplated nickel silver, from c. 1840, recently marked with crossed arrows, crossed keys, bell, hand or pineapple
Nickel silver	alloy of copper, zinc and nickel, often passed off as silver by mis-describing nickel, eg. German silver
Ormolu	gilded bronze, mostly used for mounts
Parcel gilt	silver with part coating of gold
Pewter	greyish alloy of tin with lead or other grey metal, sometimes polished, with circular seam and often no or obscure mark
Sheffield plate	copper sandwiched between layers of sterling silver and rolled into sheets for use, made from 1760-1840. Seams are dovetailed and marks, when found, are similar to hallmarks.
Silver gilt	silver with coating of gold
Silver plate	term for works in silver other than personal ornaments or coins
Silver plated	articles of metal with thin coating of silver, with manufacturer's marks only
Sterling standard	near pure silver

DECORATIVE TECHNIQUES

Applied	ornament or part applied to the surface
Basse-taille	effect of working metal in relief and overlaying enamel to give different colour shades where enamel differs in depth.
Cast	pattern made by running molten metal or pressing soft material into a mould (and the negative mould itself)
Champlevé	method of enamelling by cutting troughs from metal into which composition (frit) is melted
Chasing	effect of pushing metal into pattern without removing it, achieved by surface hammering. Common in brass.
Cloisonné	method of enamelling whereby pattern is defined by framework of enclosures (cloisons)
Embossing or Repoussé	bosses pushed into patterns from the back
Enamelling	coloured glass-like inlay

METAL

Engraving (incising)	removal of metal by scratching, commonly used for armorials (early 18th century armorials **cast, chased** or **applied**)
Finial	decorative knob on top of lid, cover or upright etc. or terminal at base of handle
Hatched	matted engraved lines, small circles or dots
Knot	protrusion on stem
Niello	engraved lines filled with black alloy
Swan-necked handle	double curving feature similar to scrolling used in description of pewter objects
Thumbpiece	finial rising from top of handle

MARKS

Metal marks generally consist of a **maker's mark**; a **metal mark**; a **date letter**; and, for gold and silver, an **Assay Office mark**. A detailed pocket guide to marks is an essential tool.

The first mark is the sponsor's or maker's mark, the second is the sterling mark, the third is the assay office, and the fourth is the date letter mark indicating the year of the Assay, which is changed annually and varies according to town of origin. The shape of the shields and the type of lettering are all vital, as are any distinguishing dots, crowns etc. Lids or attachments may have separate marks.

Sponsor or maker's mark   Sterling   Assay Office   Date letter

Sterling standard silver
Leopard's head mark (1300 - 1543), crowned leopard (1478-1543), lion passant (1544-1697 and 1720 to present day) supported by Assay Office mark (92.5 per cent silver)

Gold
leopard's head mark (1300-1543); lion passant (1544-1797); lion passant and Britannia standard (1697-1720); 18ct (1798); 15,12 & 9cts (1854); 14ct (1932); shape of date letter shield can differ from silver

Platinum
Similar assay office marks to gold and silver except standard mark (orb surmounted by cross within a pentagon), introduced in 1975

Foreign plate
Before 1800 no UK marks were added but from 1842 all imported plate sold had to be assayed. From 1883 to 1904 an F mark was added in a square with chamfered corners for gold or in a blunt oval for silver. Since 1904 the F punch has been omitted, so that pieces carry the British hall mark and Assay office mark in square or oval shields plus the decimal value of the standard.

Britannia
Standard figure of Britannia (95.8 percent silver), used from 1697 to present day, replaced sterling compulsorily from 1697-1720, thereafter optional

Lion's head Erased
Mark used in conjunction with Britannia Standard mark from 1697 until 1975, indicating London Assay Office unless another is shown.

METAL
Decoration

DECORATION

A great variety of decorative forms appear on metal items.

13th & 14th
century stamped
tendril ornament

17th & 18th
century wrought
iron waterleaf

17th & 18th
century repoussé
sheet iron acanthus

18th century cast
iron medallion

Twist

Fish tail

Ribbon end

Ribbon end scroll

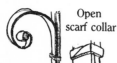

Scrolls

Open
scarf collar

Astragal
collar

Clip
collars

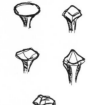

Solid barrel
or bolt end

Flat nib or
half-penny snub

Fiddlehead

Rolled nib

NAILS AND SCREWS

Tapering metal screws were first introduced in the late 17th century and were hand-filed with irregular threads. Lathe-turned screws appeared in the late 18th century and machine-made screws in the mid-19th century.

pre-1850 short
shank screw

post-1850
oval nail

17th & 18th
century hand-made
clout nails

pre-1850

post-1850 long
shank screw

post-1850
wire nail

MS

METAL

THUMBPIECES

Ramshead or
corkscrew

Volute

Scroll

Moulded

Chair

Twin lobe

Open

Pierced

Pomegranate

Bud

Hammerhead

Embryo shell

Bifurcated leaf

Bifurcated

HANDLE FINIALS

Rat tail

Fish tail

Heel

Spade

Ball

Attention

Shield

Leaf

Scroll

101

METAL
Fixtures

HINGES

The earliest metal hinges in Norman times recall Viking designs, being crescent-shaped with snake-head, tendril or flower terminals. By the 12th century hinges had become more geometrical. The greatest period for metalwork decoration was the 13th century when scrollwork was widely used, before a decline in the quality of blacksmiths' work in the 14th century.

Like handles, hinges are unreliable for dating purposes, since all styles have been copied throughout the centuries.

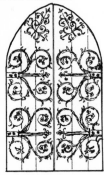

Decorative strap hinges
Horizontal straps with diverging channelled scrolled stems and leaves

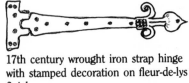

17th century wrought iron strap hinge with stamped decoration on fleur-de-lys finial

Strap hinge with incised chevron decoration and fleur-de-lys finial

Gudgeon hook smithed to a wrought iron lug over which the eye of the strap hinge sometimes passed

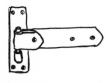

Pin hung hook and band hinge, the eye (formed by the band return) passing over a pin

T-hinge

16th & 17th century butterfly hinges

16th & 17th century cock's head hinge

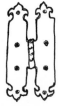

18th century
H-hinge or Parliament hinge

Butt hinge in use from c. 1680

KEYS AND LOCKS

Keys made before 1850 usually have bits filed on the front; after 1850 they are filed on the bottom edge

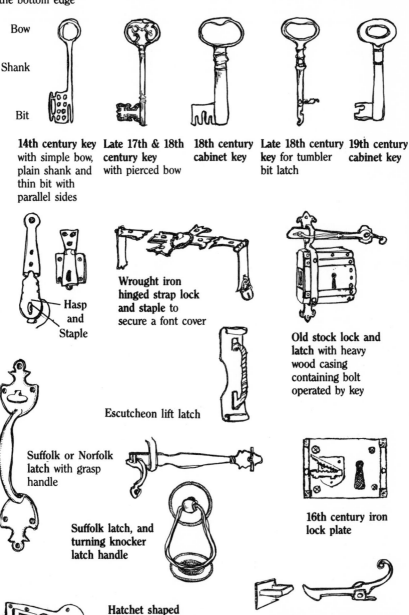

Bow

Shank

Bit

14th century key with simple bow, plain shank and thin bit with parallel sides

Late 17th & 18th century key with pierced bow

18th century cabinet key

Late 18th century key for tumbler bit latch

19th century cabinet key

METAL

Hasp and Staple

Wrought iron hinged strap lock and staple to secure a font cover

Old stock lock and latch with heavy wood casing containing bolt operated by key

Escutcheon lift latch

Suffolk or Norfolk latch with grasp handle

16th century iron lock plate

Suffolk latch, and turning knocker latch handle

Hatchet shaped latch with tumbler bit latch lock

Holdback catch for gates

METAL
Fixtures

HANDLES AND KEY ESCUTCHEONS

Although some handle shapes are typical of a particular period, all have been much copied at different times.

Keyholes on English furniture are generally rounded at the base until the 18th century.

1. Square iron lockplate with trefoil corners 14th, 15th and 16th centuries
2. Iron stirrup with cruciform backplate 16th and 17th centuries
3. Iron loop-drop twist with round backplate 16th and 17th centuries
4. Iron heart-shaped loop-drop on a shaped key escutcheon 16th and 17th centuries
5. Iron ring or dutch drop (1690-1710)
6. Cast brass pear-drop on circular moulded backplate c.1700
7. Split tail or axe-drop on hexafoil backplate early 18th century
8. Acorn drop c.1700
9. Tangs and loop on engraved and shaped backplate early 18th century
10. Shield-shaped key escutcheon, often engraved early 18th century
11. Bail handle passing through cast knobs on solid backplate c 1710
12. Bail handle passing through cast knobs on cutaway backplate c 1730
13. Bail handle passing through cast knobs on pierced backplate c 1750
14. 1740-70
15. Dutch drop from 1750
16. Swan-necked loop from 2 circular moulded backplates from 1750 and much used in the 19th century
17. Mid 18th century Chinoiserie with geometric piercing
18. Rococo with 2 separate plates for handle sockets and acanthus decoration (decoration sometimes asymmetrical) from c.1750
19. from 1770
20. Relief-stamped oval backplate with plain loop handle passing through two knobs from c. 1750
21. Circular relief-stamped handle on circular moulded backplate from c. 1770
22. Lion mask with ring 1790-1820
23. Relief-stamped swan-necked handle attached to oval rose-stamped backplates
24. Beaded circular loop attached to stamped circular backplate c. 1820
25. Sunken or recessed handle often found on military or travelling chests c.1820
26. Art nouveau fixed protruding loop c.1900

METAL
Fixtures

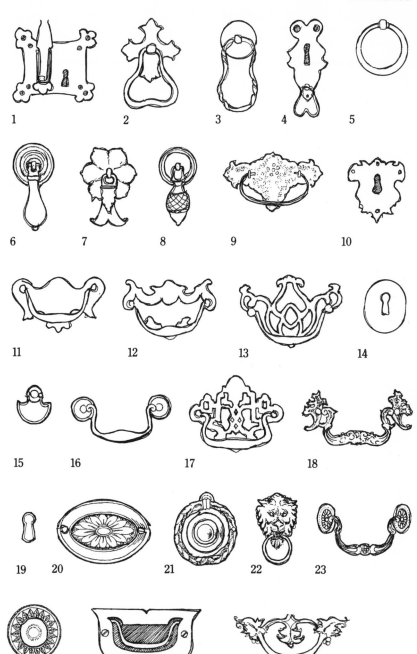

1

2

3

4

5

6

7

8

9

10

11

12

13

14

15

16

17

18

19

20

21

22

23

24

25

26

METAL

105

METAL
Religious Objects
BAPTISM, HOLY WATER, OIL AND INCENSE

Portable font
Cercelée cross with iron finial
Oak body with metal lift-out
bowl on hand-forged wrought
iron cruciform stand on oak
plinth with chamfered edges

Silver stoup or Holy Water basin
Backplate of lozenge-shaped
cartouche form with strapwork,
repoussé and hammered
decoration with Sacred
Monogram IHS in plain roman
capitals superimposed on latin
cross on central medallion
Acanthus decorated bombe
basin stepped at base
Pendant ball and steeple finial

Silver asperges bucket
Tubular lobed bale or swing
handle
Moulded floriated double
curved rim
Vase shaped body with chased
decoration of cupid's head and
festoons
Collet *(collar)* at junction of
body and foot
High domed foot with turned
over edge and matted scrolled
decoration

METAL

Asperges or holy water sprinkler
with perforated ball finial and baluster stem of silver, attached to oak handle with silver baluster knot

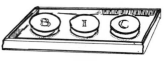

Aspergillum
brush with short silver handle

Chrismatory
containing set of holy oil stocks

Baptismal shell
with shaped silver handle on which is an engraved Maltese cross

Stem struck strainer spoon
of Old English pattern c.1730 with elliptical bowl and name of church engraved in script on handle

Incense dish of boat shape c.1742
edged with roll moulding, on baluster stem above high circular foot stepped at base
Double lid, hinged amidship, with ends of flaps secured by cast scrolled clasps projecting from bulwarks

Censer
Finial encased in cresting of loops, with 3 chains running through rising from attachments to base
Thumbpiece attached to trefoil base
Lobed hexagonal body with everted edge
Roundel applied to each lobe cusped inside with spoke pattern ending in trefoils
Hexagonal foot with double roll edge, each facet being pierced with hole for attachments.
Domed and stepped cover with lobed rim, decorated with double roll mouldings and pierced dormers

METAL
Bells

BELLS

Bells are hung in the **bell chamber**, usually high in the tower or spire of the church. The bells are rung from the **ringing chamber** and between them is a **dead chamber** or (if it contains a clock) the **clock chamber**. In the late 19th century, the Rev. Ellacombe introduced a pulley system for bell chimes which is often found and is known as the **Ellacombe Chiming System**.

Bells frequently have names, the majority feminine, but some male, like Great Tom of Oxford or Big Ben. They are stamped with foundry marks and may carry other inscriptions. The character of the lettering and the foundry marks upon old bells are valuable in determining date, although the same stamps were used for centuries and sometimes more than one foundry used the same stamp simultaneously.

Important bells may be listed for preservation by the diocese and their detailed history is often included in descriptive leaflets of the church.

Principal English Bellfoundries
1424-1513 Brasyers of Norwich, Norfolk
1506-1616 Newcombes of Leicester
1518-1709 Knights of Reading
1539-1741 Oldfields of Nottingham
1570-today The Whitechapel Bell Foundry Ltd, London (incorporating Mot; Bartlet; Phelps; Lester; Pack; Mears; Mears & Stainbank)
1584-1697 Purdues of Somerset
1590-1682 Cliburys of Wellington, Shropshire
1610-1823 Penningtons of Devon and Cornwall
1631-1782 Bagleys of Chacombe, Northamptonshire
1635-1726 Chandlers of Drayton Parslow, Buckinghamshire
1652-1731 Smiths of York
1684-1830 Rudhalls of Gloucester
1698-1814 Bilbies of Chewstoke, Somerset
1788-1809/1853-1918 John Warner & Sons, London
1800-today John Taylor & Co (Bellfounders) Ltd, Loughborough, Leicestershire

Recording note:
Always ask a trained ringer to lower the bell for examination and do not touch a bell set upside down or pull a rope attached to one. For each bell take note of the name or number; the note; the weight; the inscription; the likely date; the bellfounder; the diameter of the mouth; the presence of canons and argent; the condition (cracked or sound); and if rehung and by whom.

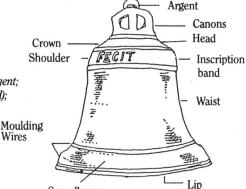

Argent
Canons
Head
Crown
Shoulder
Inscription band
Waist
Moulding Wires
Soundbow
Lip

COMMUNION OR EUCHARIST: Cups

The Communion Wine

Before the Reformation, the cup at the centre of the Eucharist was known as a chalice; after about 1525 it was known as a communion cup, but the term chalice came back into common usage towards the end of the 18th century and for 19th and 20th century cups influenced by pre-Reformation designs.

The most ornate mediaeval chalices are about 17 cm high and set with cabuchons, whereas similar 19th century examples are larger and mounted with faceted jewels.

12th and 13th century Norman chalice
Wide shallow bowl with moulded rim with everted rim
Cylindrical stem, often quite plain
Spherical knot, either lobed, wrythen *(spiral)*, plain or pierced
Circular foot with engraved or raised ornament and often stamped beading on the edge

Font cup c. 1510
Font-shaped bowl on sturdy trumpet stem with narrow cabled collet at junction of bowl and stem
Bowl annulated *(ringed)* by band with raised inscription in plain roman capitals, *COMMUNION CUP*, the words separated by tied scrolls, probably added in the 17th century

Early 16th century pre-Reformation Tudor chalice
Deep bowl with everted rim, set in star-shaped calyx *(cup-like cavity)* at each angle
Gothic knot with six lozenge bosses, each with a tracery motif on red or green enamel on the facets, amidst intervening lobes
Hexagonal lobed foot with saints in cusped niches engraved on the panels, one panel bearing an engraved crucifix

Tudor communion cup c.1574
Deep bucket-shaped bowl, annulated with band of strapwork and moresques, resting on a compressed hemispherical knot above a wide flange
Foot and base trumpet shaped, with stamped egg and dart moulding on edge

Tudor communion cup c. 1576
Deep beaker-shaped bowl with everted rim decorated with strapwork arabesque
Lozenge decorated collet joins bowl and spool stem with lozenge ornament at lower edge
Domed and stepped circular foot, the lower edge ornamented as on stem, the base encircled with gadrooning

Communion cup c.1600
Deep conical bowl, engraved with IHS across the stem of a cross, within a rayed frieze
Baluster stem
High circular foot stepped at base with ring moulding

Communion cup c. 1686
Deep beaker-shaped bowl with everted rim engraved with armorials contained within foliate ornament of two crossed branches of laurel tied below with a ribbon
Trumpet-shaped stem with narrow central flange
Shallow stepped and domed circular foot
Inscriptions at this period usually in English in lettering similar to that used on contemporary monuments

Mid-18th century communion cup

Goblet-shaped bowl annulated with applied moulding above which is an engraved IHS within rays and below inverted rays

Trumpet-shaped stem with compressed moulded knot two-thirds of the way up and engraved putti at base

Domed and stepped foot with rayed decoration

Late 18th century communion cup

Ogee-shaped bowl encircled near top with raised foliate ornament and festoons of flowers and foliage

Fluted calyx reaching halfway up the bowl

Baluster stem with spiral gadrooning

Foliated collet joining the stem to the high domed fluted foot on a spreading base which is encircled with raised acanthus leaves

Mid-19th century chalice

Hemispherical bowl annulated with lines of niello enclosing inscription in 19th century lombardic lettering

Small cast and applied calyx of fleur-de-lys

Circular stem with stepped mouldings and vertical wires and pellets *(small balls)* on a niello ground.

Gadroons and foliated mouldings decorate the knot.

Filigree scrolls on the collet.

Conical foot divided into six panels by rope mouldings each containing an applied roundel with representations of the Evangelists and other symbols

Stepped circular edge

19th century chalice inspired by Norman style

Plain conical bowl set in an arcaded calyx, with filigree decorated architrave and spandrels, the pillars set with cabuchons.

Circular stem annulated with mouldings and water leaves above and below the angular knot which is decorated with filigree scrolling and 8 stone bosses

High circular flaring stepped foot with an inverted filigree arcade, as in the calyx and filigree ornament on the edge

METAL
Religious Objects

20th century chalice
Double cone or egg-timer shape, the bowl shallower than the base
Lower third of bowl and whole stem base decorated with hammered abstract geometrical designs

Chalice
showing an amalgamation of decorative details from two silver gilt chalices of 1525 and 1527

Hemispherical bowl annulated with a band inscribed in gothic lettering on a hatched ground
CALICEM . SALUTARI . ACCIPIUM . ET . NOMEN . INVOCABI (sic)
Hexagonal collet of stepped moulding below the bowl and above the knot
Hexagonal stem, rising from balustrade with pinnacles at the angles, displaying panels of pierced quatrefoil tracery within cabling, interrupted by a large lobed gothic knot with six projecting lozenge bosses embellished with raised human masks on the facets
High hexagonal foot decorated with panels in two stages, the upper with feathering, the lower with plain lettering on a hatched ground (indecipherable)
One bell-shaped panel, protruding from the others, engraved with a crucifix, the rim of the bell curving onto the bottom step of a circular stepped flange
Wavy-edged hexagonal stepped base with stamped vertical billet decoration on the riser

THE SACRAMENT

Ciborium	covered chalice for storing the Sacrament, distinguishable from cup or chalice by rim or ledge *(bezel)* on which the cover rests
Monstrance	decorative container for Sacrament to be displayed to worshippers
Paten	plate on which the Sacrament is served during Eucharist
Pyx	box for carrying the Sacrament to the sick
Salver	plate, larger than paten, for serving Sacrament during Eucharist
Tabernacle	decorative container for the ciborium or wafer box
Tazza	wine cup with shallow circular bowl mounted on foot, often confused with patens or salvers
Wafer box	box for storing the wafers

Ciborium
Baluster finial supporting patonce cross set with a white sapphire

Slightly domed and stepped cover, *usually hallmarked*

Shaped hemispherical bowl with everted rim

Hexagonal collet at junction of bowl and hexagonal stem
Stepped collet
Wrythen pierced gothic knot bearing six lozenge bosses with raised foliate ornament set with sapphire centres

Stepped collet at junction of stem
Hexagonal incurving foot
Edge engraved with band of reeding
Six pierced trefoil toes

METAL
Religious Objects

THE SACRAMENT: Patens

Normally a simple flat decorated plate, the paten can have a foot and stem (**standing patens**) and certain 17th century covered patens are furnished with spool feet and covers and resemble ciboria. The covers of such standing patens are often an inverted copy of the base, know as **paten lids** and were used in the 16th century to double as covers for the communion cup. The base of patens are usually decorated with a button bearing a Sacred Monogram or the name of the church in a roundel.

Paten 12th to 14th century
Circular with double depression
Band contained within the moulded rim circumscribed in plain latin lombardic uncials on a hatched ground
+ *CALICEM SALUTARIS ACCIPIAM ET NOMINE DOMINE INVOCABO* with a cross at the beginning and lozenge devices between each word
Domed centre engraved with Head of Christ set in roundel within an engraved sunburst on a matted ground, all within an embossed sexfoil with spandrels engraved with small sun motifs
On the reverse, Sacred Monogram in latin form

Standing paten c.1576
Bezel to fit communion cup
Spool foot, with button on base
Button engraved horizontally with date in arabic numerals
Reeded outer edge, similar to top
Spool finial, outside annulated with a band of strapwork and moresques
Inside of paten lid undecorated with single depression and single reeded border to narrow rim, with protruding bezel

Monstrance
Silver, parcel-gilt and set with carbuncles in the form of a shrine.
Glazed crested roundel centre front to contain Sacrament, edged with rope moulding and fleurs-de-lys tracery, supported on stepped silver plinth with gilt moulding, engraved dog-tooth patterning, set with 5 carbuncles.
On each side, a buttress decorated with tracery and geometric patterns, pinnacled and crocketed, with niches containing 2 gilt figures of angels holding crowns.
Above the roundel, a gabled silver roof, with dormers, engraved with a sexfoil foliated device, set with carbuncles and with gilt cresting.
A floriated gilt cross with central carbuncle at apex of roof.
Shrine rests on hexagonal stem decorated with engraved dog-tooth and other ornament, branching at top into scrolls and crockets and edged horizontally with brattishing.
Compressed spherical knot with embossed lobes and 6 bosses, each framed in swirling crockets and set with carbuncles.
Gilt collet at junction of stem and foot.
Hexfoil foot, parcel-gilt, decorated with foliated ornament on matted ground, with carbuncles set in each foil; the base with gilt mouldings and engraved decoration

Salver c.1693 used as a paten
Narrow rim with triple reeded border
Single depression with shallow straight-sided bouge
Slight moulded collet at junction of top and high flaring foot which is edged with ovolo
decoration and stands on a narrow flanged base
Incised armorials in centre of well with marks:
London assay 1693; maker's mark PM within quatrefoil
Additional mark, lion passant, on underside of flange; 1713 incised on base

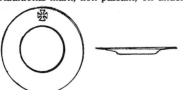

Plate paten
Broad rimmed plate with engraved patée
cross on rim
Inscription engraved in roman capitals on
back of rim

Dish paten
Saucer dish with shallow foot-rim
Hammered decoration covering inside

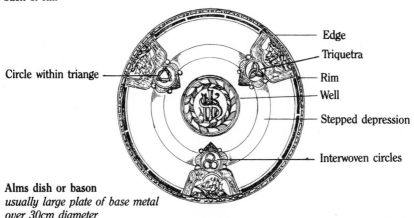

Circle within triange

Edge
Triquetra
Rim
Well
Stepped depression
Interwoven circles

Alms dish or bason
*usually large plate of base metal
over 30cm diameter*
Circular silver alms dish with enamelled decoration (40.5 cm diameter), with moulded
patterned edge to panelled rim.
3 medallions rise from bosses in stepped depression of the dish, containing embossed
representations of The Holy Trinity (triquetra; circle within triange; interwoven circles) framed
by enamelled wing forms arching back to and framing silver reliefs of sailing ships on rim.
In the centre the Sacred Monogram IHS in plain roman capitals in an enamelled roundel
within coiled rope pattern.

METAL
Religious Objects

Pyx
vessel used to carry the Sacrament to the sick, usually a box smaller than a wafer box but found in many forms.

Wafer box
with lift out grid

Pinnacled and crocketed spirelet

Open (to contain monstrance) with buttresses supporting hexagonal gabled canopy

Square base, each side with crocketed gable; door at front, decorated with raised cross

Altar tabernacle
in 3 stages

Hanging tabernacle
with veil

METAL

CROSSES

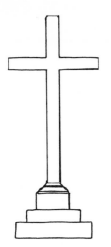

**Plain 3-stepped
latin calvary altar cross**

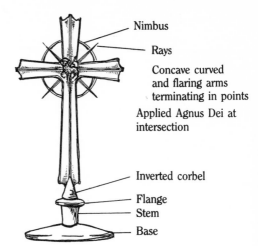

Nimbus

Rays

Concave curved
and flaring arms
terminating in points

Applied Agnus Dei at
intersection

Inverted corbel

Flange

Stem

Base

Passion altar cross

Celtic-style processional cross

Handwrought brass wheel cross with
repoussé celtic ornament on the splayed
limbs and wheel or nimbus

Central concave sided lozenge medallion
displaying Sacred Monogram IHS in plain
roman letters on a chased ground

Compressed and annulated brass knot and
cylindrical stem joins the cross to the
screw-jointed oak stem with brass ferrule
at base

Screw joint

Pectoral cross
incorporating rose and heart
emblems in gold and enamel

Brass ferrule

METAL

METAL
Religious Objects

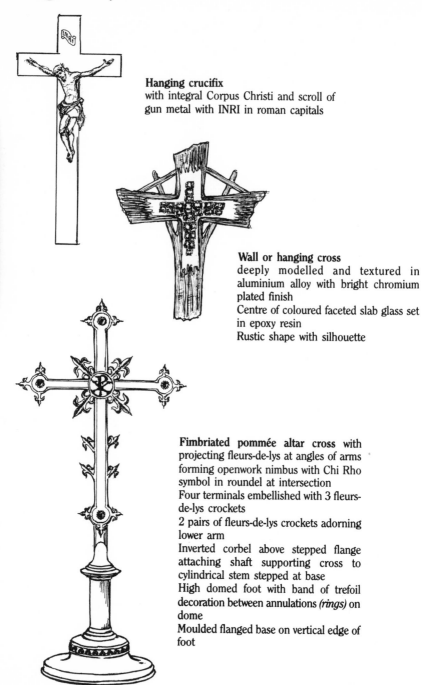

Hanging crucifix
with integral Corpus Christi and scroll of
gun metal with INRI in roman capitals

Wall or hanging cross
deeply modelled and textured in
aluminium alloy with bright chromium
plated finish
Centre of coloured faceted slab glass set
in epoxy resin
Rustic shape with silhouette

Fimbriated pommée altar cross with
projecting fleurs-de-lys at angles of arms
forming openwork nimbus with Chi Rho
symbol in roundel at intersection
Four terminals embellished with 3 fleurs-
de-lys crockets
2 pairs of fleurs-de-lys crockets adorning
lower arm
Inverted corbel above stepped flange
attaching shaft supporting cross to
cylindrical stem stepped at base
High domed foot with band of trefoil
decoration between annulations *(rings)* on
dome
Moulded flanged base on vertical edge of
foot

Mid-19th century crucifix

Arms engraved with fleurs-de-lys in diaper pattern

To each arm is attached a quatrefoil edged with roll moulding, engraved with foliage on a matted ground, set with a single amethyst

The 3 upper arms terminate in fleurs-de-lys with roll mouldings and engraved foliage centres. The intersection of the arms, outlined with gables of roll moulding but otherwise left plain as a background to the head of Christ, is surrounded by an octagon, cusped on its inner side, concave on its outer and crested on the 4 exposed angles with fleurs-de-lys, the width filled with a band of dog-tooth ornament between roll mouldings on a hatched ground.

An inverted corbel is placed at the junction of the cross and the knot of the annulated cylindrical stem *(for figure see page 53)*

The compressed annulated spherical knot has 4 bosses bearing applied roundels of fleurs-de-lys on blue enamel

The high tapering foot, with 4 shaped lobes, is engraved with the Sacred Monogram IHS in a roundel and a running pattern of trefoils

An engraved band of hatching occupies the space between the edge of the foot and base

The wooden frame of the cross is cased on the front in plates of base metal, the base of electroplated base metal and the figure of Christ is electrogilt

METAL
Preaching

PREACHING
Lecterns became a feature of post-Reformation churches, usually very austere and made up of an amalgamation of different decorative parts. From the beginning of the 19th century lecterns became more simple. **Book stands** are particularly used to support the priest's **missal** during services.

Brass lectern c. 1683
Book desk in form of eagle with outstretched wings flanked by single bracket candle holders with glass tulip-shaped shades
Sphere
Flaring concave stem above various bands of moulding including some raised leaf work
Baluster stem with stepped circular base
Cylindrical section springing from stepped moulding
High domed lectern base resting on four lion sejant feet

Late 19th century brass lectern with restored iron feet
Double desk with gable ends pierced with cusped circular openings and band of cresting across top
Cylindrical stem decorated with rings of red and blue inlaid mastic with formalised leaf forms supporting desk
Central compressed spherical knot with attached band with knobbed decoration, scalloped edges and trefoil collets above and below
Trefoil collet at junction of stem and base
Conical base decorated with pierced sexfoils and rings of red and blue inlaid mastic standing on 4 red painted paw feet protruding from cusped edge

Pedestal missal or book stand
in highly polished brass with revolving
bookplate embellished with pierced
quatrefoils within roundels in corners and
central roundel with sacred monogram
IHS in latin form on punched ground
Rope moulded edge to bookplate,
screwjoint and trumpet base

METAL

Ledger missal or book stand
with cast scrolled and foliated end panels
and scalloped edge to bookplate ledge

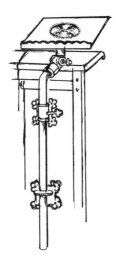

Pulpit desk
with quatrefoil decoration in centre and
a scalloped ledge
Adjustable stem (by use of key) attached
to inside of pulpit drum by clips to square
bracket plates with trefoil corners

METAL
Religious Objects

PROCESSIONAL

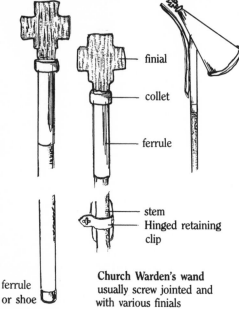

finial

collet

ferrule

stem
Hinged retaining clip

ferrule
or shoe

Church Warden's wand
usually screw jointed and
with various finials

Verger's wand
similar to Church Warden's but shorter

Candle extinguisher and taper
Brass cone-shaped extinguisher with
rolled edge and patée cross finial and
bent cylindrical taper holder attached
by brass ferrule to oak stem

Pax
tablet with projecting carrying
handle behind, decorated
on front with **rood** or sacred
symbol

Morse
*badge sewn or pinned to band joining sides of cope,
sometimes embroidered but usually metal*
Holy Trinity in basse-taille enamel on silver with pierced
gold outer rim

Pastoral staff or crozier
Silver gilt, decorated with enamels and semi-precious stone
Hexagonal crook, imbricated and set with stones, terminating
in serpent's head with forked tongue, connected to stem of
foliated ornament by curve of tongue
Central figures of Christ (standing) charging St Peter (seated)
on an enamelled ground
4 Marks above niches, maker's mark, sterling standard, Assay
Office and date
2 tiers of niches flanking stem, separated by pinnacled
buttresses, occupied by figures of saints and bishops under
foliated canopies: upper tier surmounted by 3 figures standing
against alternate facets of the hexagonal stem
Plinth of lower tier of niches set on foliated boss rising by a
concave stem from knot decorated with swirling gadroons
Shield, bearing arms of See, set on ferrule at top of oak staff

GATES AND RAILINGS

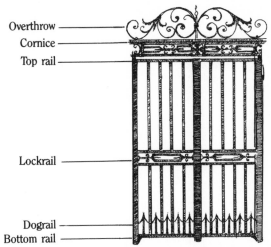

Overthrow
Cornice
Top rail

Lockrail

Dograil
Bottom rail

17th century wrought iron gates (pair)

Overthrow of 2 large bifurcated S scrolls, passing through central collar and decorated with small scrolls including fiddle head, flat penny nibs and pair of well placed waterleaves
Frieze of strapwork between 2 square section rails below cornice
Plain square section top rail
Double lockrail with strapwork frieze
Plain square section bottom rail with dograil of arrowheads
In each gate there are 4 square section verticals, between unadorned stiles, the verticals being morticed, tenoned and welded through the horizontals

16th century wrought iron tomb railing
Fleur-de-lys alternating with spiked finials to the uprights which change to flat section above the toprail
Main verticals with ball and steeple finials, ornamented with double bar twist below the toprail

METAL
Practical Objects

Candlesticks

17th century pewter candlestick
Bell-shaped

17th century brass candlestick
Vertical slot in cylindrical stem with protruding candle ejector
Drip pan in centre of stem
Wide spreading base

Late 17th century silver or gilt baroque candlestick
Gadrooned drip pan and pricket
Baluster stem shaped and ornamented
Scroll tripod base surmounted by putti

Classical silver candlestick c.1675
Fluted reeded column of doric form with broad platform at base
High waisted plinth
Large square stepped foot

Early 18th century silver or brass candlestick
Steel rod ejector in base
Reel-shaped sconce on distinct neck
Shouldered baluster stem with knots
Moulded and depressed polygonal foot

Neo-classical silver or brass late 18th century candlestick
Tapering fluted stem
High trumpet-shaped foot
Bell shaped leaf - decorated sconce with separate nozzle

METAL

Nozzle and drip pan scalloped, with deep indentations between each pair of scallops, annulated with two pairs of incised rings

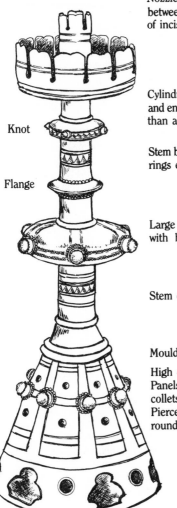

Cylindrical stem with 3 knots, the upper one gem set and engraved with zigzag ornament, the lower little more than a flange

Knot

Stem between them annulated by double rows of incised rings enclosing a zigzag pattern

Flange

Large compressed central knot, chased and decorated with bead mouldings and with stones as bosses

Stem decorated as above, with rings and zigzag

Moulded collets

High conical foot
Panels formed of chased fillets with stones set in high collets
Pierced cusped openings alternating with pierced roundels

19th century copper gilt altar candlestick set with semi-precious stones

Five-branch candelabrum

Brass flat-scrolled branches with ivy leaf repoussé ornament springing from top of cylindrical stem, holding shallow saucer-shaped grease-pans with scalloped cresting and annulated cylindrical nozzles

Central fifth socket at top of reeded rod with scrolling brackets

Polychrome imbricated iron stem with brass terminal ferrule passing through collar of base and joined, by a brass knot, at top to a brass cylindrical stem

Wrought iron base formed of broken scrolled legs with ribbon ends, united by wide incurving collar with bolt-end terminals

Seven branch
jerusalem candlestick
or menorah

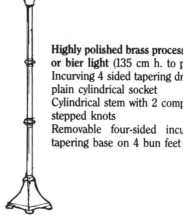

Highly polished brass processional torch or bier light (135 cm h. to pan)

Incurving 4 sided tapering drip pan with plain cylindrical socket

Cylindrical stem with 2 compressed and stepped knots

Removable four-sided incurving and tapering base on 4 bun feet

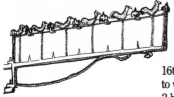

16th century wrought iron bracket of prickets, attached to wall and pivoted

2 horizontal bars, connected by spiral uprights, forming 5 open panels with spike at midpoint of base of each as support for candle which passes through ring in upper bar, crested with alternating fleurs-de-lys and cocks

Strap sconce

Rushlight holder

Flowerstand
(adapted from torchere)
Disc top with embattled gallery
Twist stem joined by spindle collet to rectangular section supported by scrolled cruciform bracket feet united to stem by clip collars in 3 places

14th century wrought iron herse (top) erected around or over tombs for their protection with fleur-de-lys decorated candle prickets

METAL
Practical Objects

Hanging lights

Lanterns and chandeliers in churches were used to supplement candlesticks from around 1600, first plain English chandeliers and later in the century, more ornate dutch examples.

The commonest shape of 17th century chandelier has drooping branches hooked into rings in the balusters or into trays pierced with holes. The branches are mostly circular in section and of two opposed curves with moulding at the join, so that the inner end forms an open spiral and the outer end is everted. The finial at the top was often highly decorative and different provincial centres had their own characteristic finials.

During the 18th century, the arms became shorter, drooped less and were fitted to the circumference of a flatter central sphere. The branches themselves were more elaborate, often hexagonal or octagonal and covered with scrolling. The spaces between the branches and tiers were filled with ornament, usually gadrooning and the most popular finial was a flame.

Dutch chandeliers in the 18th century had no finials or ornament and the branches were attached to hollow trays by tenons and pins, rather than hooks.

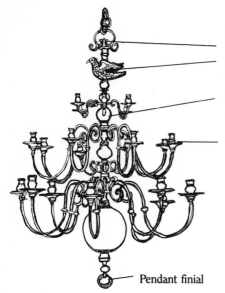

Brass chandelier of mixed date
Top finial
London dove finial
Bristol dove has closed wings and no feathers on body
Shaft of ball and baluster turnings (hollow and held together with iron rod)

Tiers of curving branches, usually 2 or 3

Pendant finial

Oil lamp with clear glass chimney and opaque china hemispherical cover
3 wrought iron broken-scrolled brackets suspended from iron linked chains
Brass body fitting into annulated iron girdle

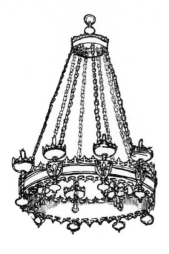

Wrought iron corona lucis
Hanging by chains from circlet crested with fleurs-de-lys
Bowl drip pans under 8 candle sockets similarly ornamented and attached to outer side of coronet by twist stems with pendant turnip-shaped finials, the joins hidden by applied fleur-de-lys decorated shields, painted red and gold
Rims of annulated coronet decorated with fleurs-de-lys

Sanctuary lamp
Highly polished brass with cast finely modelled dolphin arms attached:
by tails to ball and baluster pendant finial of drip pan;
by snouts to socket of cylindrical ruby glass 8 day candle funnel with everted lip rests;
by dorsal fins to 3 chains hanging from brass circlet surmounted with ring
Pendant finial with ring

Recording note:
Describe the shape and ornament of every part and the way the light is fitted together. For chandeliers, record the number of tiers and the number of branches in each tier, and the finials.

METAL
Practical Objects
BRACKET LIGHTS

Brass candle sconce
Cartouche-shaped sconce with repoussé decoration and central uninscribed cartouche, lower part reeded and fluted
Simple knotted s-shaped arm of round section springing from floriated boss at base, holding plain saucer-shaped drip pan with annulated cylindrical nozzle moulded at rim

Brass candle bracket
Horizontal rod of square section interrupted by twists, emerging from fleurette on backplate, supported above and below by inward scrolling waterleaf brackets, terminating in trefoil
Floral collar near terminal threaded with stem of urn-shaped socket

19th century wrought iron hexagonal porch lantern
Baluster finial with attached ring
Double domed cover with ogee ribs and scrolled lower edge, pierced panels with whorls (lower dome) and lozenges (upper dome)
Band with rectangular piercing between domes
Tapering glazed panels with iron traceried glazing bars in heads fixed to scrolled crested upper rail with band of pierced arcading between scroll and scrolled lower edge of cover
Pendant finial of scrolled brackets radiating from centre to plain moulded outside edges of bottom rail of glazed panels

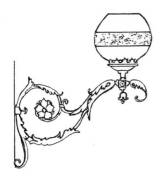

Brass bracket gasolier
Band of floral engraving on globe sitting in trefoil crested
socket with acorn pendant finial
Waterleaf scrolled arm with cast brass
fleurette inner terminal to scroll-end
near wall plate
Scroll end linked to waterleaf stem

METAL

Sanctuary bracket lamp
Bright polished chromium plate with glass
funnel nestling in calyx above disc set on
flaring reeded stem sitting in collar at end
of shaped triangular wall bracket

Processional torch
Chromium plated brass torch on teak stem
with clear glass cylindrical funnel
Handle grip of textured brass to prevent
it slipping through collar of wall mounted
bracket

METAL
Practical Objects

TANKARDS, FLAGONS AND JUGS

Beaker   shaped, lipped vessel without a handle or stem
Cup   term applied to any form of drinking vessel in old documents
Flagon   large vessel from which other vessels are filled
Mug   cylindrical drinking vessel without lid
Tankard   drinking vessel with handle and hinged lid

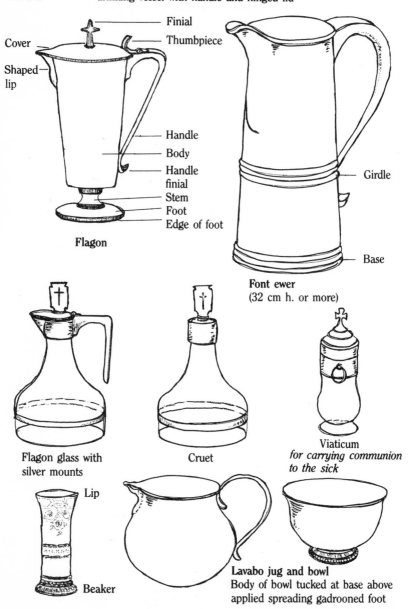

Finial
Cover
Thumbpiece
Shaped lip
Handle
Body
Handle finial
Stem
Foot
Edge of foot

Flagon

Girdle
Base

Font ewer
(32 cm h. or more)

Flagon glass with silver mounts

Cruet

Viaticum
for carrying communion to the sick

Lip

Beaker

Lavabo jug and bowl
Body of bowl tucked at base above applied spreading gadrooned foot

METAL

Silver flagon c. 1630
Flat cap lid with moulded thumbpiece pierced with heart motif
2 marks only (assay and date)
Tall cylindrical body with boldly cast lip, engraved on front with armorials and inscription in contemporary script
3 marks by handle (sterling, assay and date)
Hollow scroll handle of tapering form with simple shield-shaped finial
Spreading skirt foot with moulded band above

Tapering cylindrical pewter tankard c. 1670
Reeded flat-topped raised and stepped cover with rim extended in front and edge serrated
Corkscrew thumbpiece
Swan-necked handle with applied rat tail terminal
Continuous panel of floriated decoration
Applied girdle where base of handle meets raised body
Narrow slightly convex reeded base

19th century flagon with electrogilt mounts

High domed mount attached to hinged cover (with trefoil thumbpiece) decorated with row of tracery edged with rope moulding and cresting of trefoils surrounding wire-work nest supporting pelican in her piety

Plain lip, triangular in section projecting from band of engraved vine ornament

Scroll handle with mouchette tracery in roundel and bifurcated terminal

Upper mount annulated with roll moulding and pendant cut-card fleurs-de-lys below frieze of quatrefoil tracery surmounted in inscription *CHRIST SO LOVED US* in plain roman capitals enclosed by roll mouldings on hatched ground

Engraved metal roundel edged with cut-card trefoils enclosing the Sacred Monogram IHS on front of pear-shaped ruby glass body between mounts which encase upper and lower parts

Lower mount annulated with roll moulding surmounted by cut-card fleurs-de-lys

High quatrefoil foot with moulded edge engraved with crosses within roundels, hatched as for inscription

Hourglass stands

17th century
swordrest

Dog tongs

METAL

COINS AND MEDALS
Both the side with the monarch's head (**obverse**) and the decorative side (**reverse**) are of interest and can be recorded with a rubbing

JEWELLERY
Jewels set in 19th and 20th century church plate are likely to be facetted whereas earlier gems are usually cabuchons.

Cabuchon	stone of rounded natural form, polished but not cut
Cameo	two layers of glass, the top layer cut in relief to reveal the underlayer
Carbuncle	bright red stone
Facet	one side of cut gem
Filigree	gold or silver wire or pellets applied to gold or silver base in ornamental patterns
Girandoles	openwork clasps of alternating ribbon and bow design set with stones
Intaglios	gems with incised design

PAPER
Prints and Paintings

A miscellany of objects in churches may be made of paper or have paper as their chief material. In addition, certain framed objects dealt with under WOOD, for example, **The Roll of Honour**, may in fact appear on paper. Paintings are dealt with here though their chief material is most often canvas not paper.

FRAMED OBJECTS

All kinds of framed paper objects will be found in churches, invariably hung on the wall. The most interesting features of all framed objects will be the name of the artist, the date of the work, its subject matter and, in the case of maps and architectural drawings, its scale.

Architectural drawings	give vital clues to changes in the church's development and make interesting comparison with contemporary appearance.
Drawings and watercolours	often of religious scenes, of the church, or local landscape.
Certificates	usually framed
List of vicars	often framed manuscript or may be painted wood or stone
Painting	most likely to be copy of religious work, sometimes well known, in ornate frame
Photographs	not always carefully preserved, but the date, sitter and photographer may be interesting
Prints	impression in ink on paper, usually framed but may be unframed. Prints are often engravings taken from contemporary works of art, in which case the artist's name will be given alongside the engraver's
Roll of Honour	list of members of parish who fought in World War I 1914-18 and World War II 1939-45, usually framed and glazed and sometimes illuminated with regimental badges
Stamps	often found amongst faculties and correspondence, most interesting when attached to envelopes with indication of date.
Vignette	picture without defined borders

PRINTS

Technical terms used in the lettering are usually in Latin or French with abbreviations and contemporary spelling. There are three main recognisable types:

Intaglio	line, stell, stipple, engraving, etching, dry point and acquatint
Relievo	woodcuts and wood engravings
Lithographic	*(planographic)* resembling a drawing made with a very soft pencil

TERMS

Laid down	prints pasted on paper
Original engraving	engraving by the artist
Proof	signed by the artist and the engraver
Proof before letters	unsigned, the name of the artist and engraver printed
Lettered proof	title of subject, name of artist, engraver and publisher printed

INSCRIPTIONS

Dileneavit figuravit dessine	drawn by
Incidit sculpsit fecit	engraved by
Composuit	designed by
Excudit formit	printed by
Pinxit, peint or à la guasche	painted by

136

Books and bookbinding

Most church documents are now deposited in the county record office, where enquirers can usually view them on request. A series of books, mostly in current use, will, however, be kept in the church, in the church chest, belfry or vestry, or possibly in the rectory.

BOOKS AND PUBLICATIONS FOUND IN CHURCHES

Faculty	authorisation from Diocesan office for alteration or addition to the church, giving date and names of architect/designer, donor and materials
Library	many churches have a library of ecclesiastical works
Minute book	record of parish council meetings
Missal	service book used by priest
Register	record of births, marriages and deaths, sometimes in the same volume
Terrier	record of lands, goods and possessions of parish church
Visitors' book	record of visitors to the church from outside the parish
Other books	register of services; gift books; war memorial books; village histories; bibles; prayer books; sheet music; descriptive leaflets; parish magazines

TERMS

Association copy	book associated by ownership or annotation with the author, or with someone in connection with the author or the contents
Back	spine of book
Bands	ridges on spine caused by the sewing cords or added for decoration
Binding	outside cover
Blind tooled	impressions, without gold infill, made with tools
Boards	sides of bound or cased book
Bolts	folds which have to be cut before pages can be read
Cancels	pages containing errors (usually removed) and corrected pages
Cartouche	loosely applied to round, oval or decorated labels
Case-bound	binding method whereby boards and spine are made separately before being attached to the body of the book by the pasting down of end-papers; the basic method of modern book production
Colophon	in early printed books, a statement of the printer's name, date and place of publication usually found at end and later superseded by title page
Deckle	rough natural edge of hand-made paper
Dedication copy	presented by author to person to whom the book is dedicated
Dentelle	border with lacy pattern on inner edge
Doublure	endpapers of leather, silk or other material
Endpapers	leaves of plain and ornamental paper added by binder at front and back

PAPER
Books and bookbinding

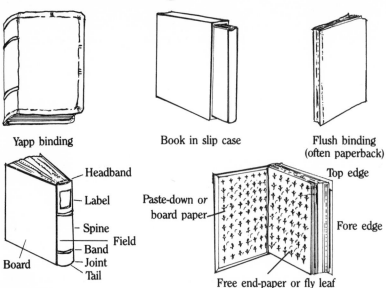

Yapp binding   Book in slip case   Flush binding
(often paperback)

Headband
Label
Spine
Band — Field
Joint
Tail
Board

Paste-down or board paper
Top edge
Fore edge
Free end-paper or fly leaf

BINDINGS

Armorial binding	stamped with coat of arms, possibly added to at later date. Royal arms do not necessarily denote royal ownership, even if the book is dedicated to a royal personage
Calf	smooth, without grain, can be variously treated and coloured
Cathedral binding	gothic architectural decoration often including rose window (1810-40)
Cottage binding	gable discernible at top and bottom in decoration (1660-1770)
Etruscan	classical decoration
Fanfare style	decoration of interlacement
Forel	parchment dressed to look like vellum
Irish	paper lozenge label in centre of board
Mosaic	polychrome decoration of binding by use of paint, onlays or inlays
Parchment	usually sheep or goat, prepared for writing or painting
Publishers cloth	apart from paperback, the usual style of commercial binding, introduced in 1823
Rococo	c-shaped curves and shell decoration popular in late 1770's and 1780's
Russia Leather	rich, smooth cowhide, scented, often decorated with blind lozenge pattern
Scots binding	wheel pattern
Signed binding	binder or designer's name or initials incorporated in or forming part of design
Sombre binding	black leather, tooled in blind, popular 1675-1725
Spanish Calf	bold dashes of red and green acid on calf binding
Tree calf	calf binding with sides stained to resemble tree or foliage
Vellum	very fine parchment or calf

PAPER

Fillet	tooled line on cover
Finishing	lettering and decoration
Fly-leaf	blank page at beginning or end
Folio (Fo)	leaf of paper folded once, usually more than 45 cm high
Fore-edge	front edge; fore-edged paintings show when the fore-edge is spread out
Format	statement indicative of shape, size and make-up of book, eg. octavo, folio etc.
French grooves	deep concave joints between spine and boards
Gauffering	gilt edges decorated with finishing tools
Guards	folded strips of paper sewn or pasted into the back during re-binding
Gutter	spine margin
Head and Tail	top and bottom of spine
Head piece	printed ornament or illustration at head of chapter or section
Headband	ornamental beading sometimes worked in silk thread at head and tail
Headcap	leather at top and tail of spine, drawn out to cover the headband
Hollow-backed	binding method where the covering material is attached to the spine by means of a hollow paper tube
Horae or Book of Hours	manuscript or printed collection of prayers for private use
Horn book	leaf of paper protected by thin plate of translucent horn and mounted on wooden tablet with handle; used for teaching children from 16th to 18th centuries
Inscribed	copy autographed by the author, usually at the request of the owner
Label (skiver)	thin pieces of morocco (even on a calf book) with lettering. From 1750 paper labels were applied to paper spines.
Limited edition	usually individually numbered
Manuscript	book or document written by hand
Marbling	process of colouring paper of edges in variegated patterns based on patterns in marble
Mint condition	as good as new
Octavo (8vo)	leaf of paper folded 3 times, i.e into 8, usually between 15 & 25 cm high
Panel	rectangle formed of single or multiple fillets, gilt or blind, on boards or between bands on spine
Panel stamped	leather bindings decorated in blind with engraved blocks process
Perfect bound	extensively used in modern books, where leaves are not sewn in sections held together by adhesive (also called **glue-back**)
Plate	illustration printed on different paper from the text. The painter or engraver will be particularly interesting
Presentation copy	spontaneous gift of the author, the value lying in the interest of the recipient or his connection with the author
Provenance	pedigree of book's previous ownership

PAPER

PAPER
Books and bookbinding

Quarto (4to)	leaf of paper folded twice, ie. into 4, usually between 25 & 40 cm high
Recto	right hand page
Repairs	books may be re-backed, re-joined, re-margined, re-set
Rotulus	book in roll form
Sections or signatures	folded sheets of paper, usually of 4 or 8 leaves or multiples thereof, from which the book is made up
Semis	repeating pattern made with small tools *(seme)*
Sprinkled	small specks on edges of leaves or on calf bindings, usually dull red
Tail piece	printed ornament or illustration at end of chapter or book
Tight-backed	binding method in which spine is attached directly to the back of the sections
Title page	page at beginning giving particulars of title, subject, authorship, publication etc.
Tooling	decoration of cover by hand tools
Uncut	edges left uncut by rebinding (not to be confused with **bolts** or **unopened**)
Unopened	edges left uncut
Verso	left hand page
Vignette	vine tendril decoration on title page
Watermark	mark in paper visible when held to light and helpful in dating printing
Wrappered book	paper binding, not hardback book in dust wrapper

Abbreviations

aeg	all edges gilt
MS.	manuscript *(pl. MSS.)*
teg	top edge gilt
nd	no date on title page
al/als	autographed letter *(ie. in the hand of the writer)/* signed autographed letter
an/ans	autographed note/ signed autographed note
ad/ads	autographed document/ signed autographed document

Full bound

Half bound

Quarter bound

Three-quarters bound

Books and bookbinding

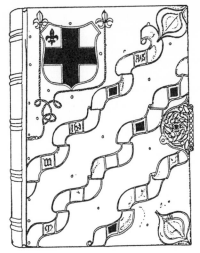

Red leather binding: with silver panels on both covers

Upper cover: 3 bands of spiralling ribbon decoration with moulded edges and set with enamels bearing Sacred Monograms on copper (all much worn), descending diagonally from R to L.

On top L corner, an enamelled shield with coat of arms (arg. a cross gu. in dexter chief a fleur de lys az.) surrounded by rope moulding with fleur de lys finials flanking the shield at the top

Raised lobed bosses at top and bottom R corners

Lower cover: 8 inset enamels on copper

In top R corner an enamelled swan with motto below, surrounded by rope moulding

Raised lobed bosses at top and bottom L corners

Brass clasp with roundel of mouchette tracery on upper cover

BIBLES:

Every church will have at least one copy of the Bible, it is most likely to be one of the following:

Great Bible 1539 -1541, 7 editions, re-printing ceased 1569

Cranmer's Bible 1540, long preface by Archbishop Cranmer

Breeches Bible 1560, roman type, see Genesis, chap.III, v.7

Authorised Version 1611

Revised Version 1881, 1884, 1895 (parts)

Two Version edition 1900

Recording note: *Essential information is author, title, place of publication (if other than London) publisher and date. Note the illustrator, format, page height, binding, inscriptions and other marks if the volume is of special interest.*

Format:

(for book) A N AUTHOR, Title of book, Publisher, Town, Date

(for article in journal) A N AUTHOR, 'Title of article', Title of journal, vol. xxx, 1976, pp. 36-41

(for information taken from a church leaflet)

Name and location of church, nth edition, 1977

STONE
Terms

Churches were often the earliest stone buildings in the community. The majority are still stone built, although other materials, such as brick, flint or concrete, have been used for churches where they are common as a local building material or where fashion demands. Decorative features found in stone will be similar in other building materials.

Ornamental stonework is often an important aspect of the decoration of a church, so that, although much of the appropriate terminology is strictly architectural *(see ARCHITECTURE)*, identification should be easier by reference to stone features in this chapter. Certain features, including **pulpits**, **feretories** and **screens**, are more likely to be wooden than stone in Britain and are therefore treated in the chapter on *WOOD*.

Aumbry	cupboard, usually for sacred vessels, in north wall of chancel
Chamfer	the narrow surface formed when an angle is cut away obliquely. It may be moulded, concave (hollow), sunk or stopped.
Credence	table or shelf by the altar, usually on the south side
Easter sepulchre	canopied recess in north chancel wall, similar to a tomb chest, used to contain the Sacrament or effigy of Christ between Good Friday and Easter Morning. Occasionally of wood.
Mensa	stone altar incised with five consecration crosses
Pillar piscina	piscina on pillar, freestanding or against wall
Piscina	basin with drain, used for washing sacred vessels, set into wall, sill or floor south of altar
Sedilia	seats for clergy, generally on south side of chancel
Squint	aperture pierced through wall to allow view of altar
Stoup	recess or niche for holding holy water near entrance to church

Stone brackets for statues or statuettes

Pillar piscina

Corbel

Credence shelf

Cresset stone
Stone with cup-like hollows filled with oil and floating wicks to give light for those performing night duties in church
(rare today)

Mensa

STONE

Aumbry

Bread oven

Piscina

Squint

**14th century
Easter sepulchre**
Canopied recess of 3 bays
with crocketed, pinnacled
and cusped ogee arches,
above a plinth resembling
a tomb chest with 4
panels of similar blind
arcaded decoration.
Adjacent on the west side
is a floor level tomb
recess of similar date and
style

14th century sedilia in
range with **piscina**.
Cusped cinquefoiled ogee
heads with crockets and
finials
Detached cylindrical
shafts, with moulded
capitals and bases,
separating 3 stepped
seats and piscina

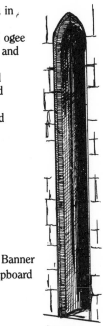

13th century sedilia

Statue niche (empty)

**Banner
cupboard**

STONE
Fonts

Saxon drum or tub font
with lead-lined bowl decorated with crudely carved
Latin crosses within arcading
Two bands of cable moulding above the stepped
base

Norman pedestal font with square bowl,
in form of capital with roundels containing carved
patterns alternating with large heads at corners.
Short octagonal stem springing from drum pedestal
on octagonal plinth
Remains of iron staple on rim for locking flat cover

Norman font with cup bowl,
elaborately carved with chevron around rim and with
patterns and stiff leaf on body, supported on massive
central cylindrical stem
4 angle shafts, rising from square plinth, outside
the bowl, support projecting masks against the
sides of top of bowl

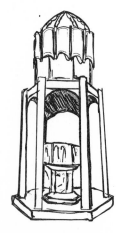

Mediaeval stone font and stone canopy
Canopy, supported on six shafts standing on an
hexagonal plinth, has high dome, decorated ribs and
is encircled by reeded panelling
Font has hexagonal bowl and stem, standing on
stepped hexagonal base in centre of plinth

Late 19th century font (1873),
copied from 15th century font
Octagonal bowl with carved representations of the 4 Evangelists and their attributes,
alternating with kneeling angels, each under crocketed ogee canopy in panels.
Bosses of demi-angels at points of intersection beneath pinnacled buttresses which separate
the panels
Octagonal stem ornamented with shields bearing symbols of the Passion on panels between
engaged shafts
Oakleaf motifs in coved section beneath bowl.
The moulded bases of the shafts stand on a stepped octagonal plinth standing on
large stepped and moulded cruciform plinth of Mansfield stone

TEXTILES
Terms

All sorts of textiles are encountered in churches, some connected with church ritual, others with decoration or even the comfort of the congregation. Vestments are dealt with under *COSTUME* but all other ecclesiastical textiles, including cloths, veils and kneelers are considered here.

Since textiles in churches often involve work of devotion, specialist techniques, particularly embroidery and tapestry, are common on small scale objects like kneelers and on large scale objects like wall hangings, popular in modern churches, Fine quality materials were used for textiles in churches from the earliest times.

TYPES OF CLOTH

Brocade	silk, cotton or synthetic cloth woven with a raised pattern of polychrome
Cloth of gold	fabric with gold thread woven into the cloth
Cloth of silver	fabric with silver thread woven into the cloth
Cotton	cloth woven from imported cotton
Damask	self coloured and patterned silk or cotton
Garniture	fringes, tassels, knots, cords, etc
Lace	fine open fabric made by hand or machine
Linen	cloth woven from flax
Lurex	20th century imitation gold thread
Silk	cloth woven from the pupae case of the silk worm
Suede	pigskin, common in 20th century applique work
Velvet	pile fabric of silk, cotton, wool or synthetics

DECORATIVE TECHNIQUES

Applied	one material laid over another
Crewel work	decorative embroidery with coloured wools on plain linen or twill ground
Embroidery	stitching in silks into pattern on cloth; canvas-work embroidery may look similar to tapestry
Gold embroidery	
purl:	threads coiled into tight spring
bullion:	large purl;
passing:	thread overlaid to resemble wire;
pearl/purl:	thread coiled into tiny gold beads;
plate:	attached flat pieces of gold;
spangles:	thin pieces of pierced metal
Gros-point	canvas work embroidery in wool using short satin stitches
Inlaid	fitting together different pieces to form a pattern
Outline work	embroidery technique of outlining pattern with couched gold cord or double thread, common with gold embroidery
Patchwork	similar to inlaid but with symmetrical pieces
Petit-point	canvas-work embroidery in strands of wool using small short satin stitches; neater than gros-point
Quilting	two or more layers of material held together by stitched pattern, sometimes with cord inserted
Raised work	padded or stumpwork stitching where embroidery is laid over padding or couching
Tapestry	weaving coloured threads into a pattern or scene

EMBROIDERY STITCHES

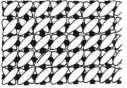

Cross

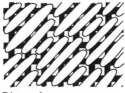

Diagonal

Diagonal satin

Eye

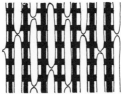

Florentine

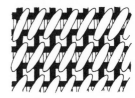

Gobelin

Holbein or double running

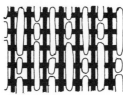

Hungarian

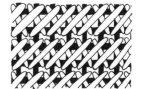

Italian

Mosaic

Parisian

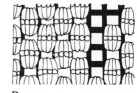

Plait

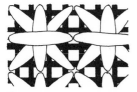

Quilting

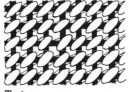

Rice

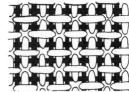

Rococo

Smyrna

Tent

Upright cross

147

TEXTILES
Embroidery

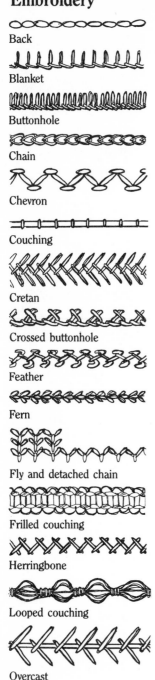

Back

Blanket

Buttonhole

Chain

Chevron

Couching

Cretan

Crossed buttonhole

Feather

Fern

Fly and detached chain

Frilled couching

Herringbone

Looped couching

Overcast

Cutwork

Darned netting

Drawn thread

Fishbone

Laid work

Openwork filling

Parted couching

Pekinese

Rosette chain

Roumanian

Satin

Split

Stem

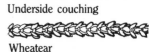
Triple cretan

Underside couching

Wheatear

Pattern darning

Embroidered cope

of red silk damask with applied crimson velvet, gold braid, green silk and canvas embroidered with gold thread, gold cord and silk in shades of green, red, yellow and brown, inlaid and couched work with metal spangles, the ground is powdered with fleur-de-lys, sunbursts, stylised pineapples and scrolled foliage and the letter P surmounted by a crown
On the false orphreys are roundels containing at centre back a Tudor rose and down the sides, the initials S P (St Paul)

On the round hood, which is attached by five silk and gold thread buttons and fringed with gold thread and red silk, is an applied roundel with the Sacred Monogram IHC within rays. The same device appears on the morse.

TEXTILES
Lace

Most church lace is machine lace of the late 19th and early 20th centuries or 19th century hand-made lace applied to machine-made net. Earlier laces, however, were given to churches at the end of the 19th century and it is worth looking out for 17th century needle laces and 18th century bobbin laces. Machine-made lace was first introduced in the late 18th century.

Needlepoint lace

Developed from drawn thread work, needlepoint lace is made with a single thread and needle, using embroidery stitches, dominated by buttonhole stitch.

Ecclesiastical robes and textiles are often adorned with rose-point, one of the many types of needlepoint, which consists of patterns worked in relief like sculptured work, forming strong and solid flowers and scrolls held in position by **brides** *(bars or ties)* enriched with **picots.**

Pillow lace

Developed from knotted fringe and network, pillow lace is made with a multitude of threads wound upon bobbins stuck into a pillow. The lace is created in a range of twists and plaits combining a varying number of threads, usually in or applied to a meshed ground. Where there is no ground **(fond or reseau)** the pattern is connected by **brides.**

Brides	bars or ties
Footing	straight edge or flouncing attached to material
Heading	scalloped or dentate free edge
Picots	small loops of twisted thread
Tallies	square or rectangular linking, characteristic of Buckinghamshire lace
Wheat ears	round or oval linking

CLOTHS

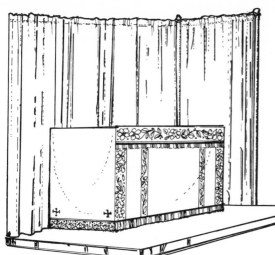

Dossal
hanging back panel

Riddel
curtain hung on riddel-posts at back and sides of altar

Super frontal
embroidered and fringed

Frontal
panelled (orphreys) and fringed

Fair linen cloth with lace edging and embroidered crosses

Laudian
3 or 4 sided throw-over altar frontal with motif on one side only

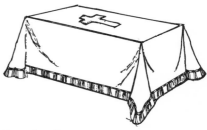

Funeral pall
usually purple or white, with motif in centre or on all sides, sometimes corners are slit

TEXTILES
Veils and Cloths

VEILS

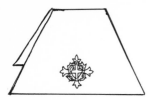

Chalice veil
square veil used to cover communion chalice when not in use

Ciborium or pyx veil
white circular veil with hole in centre under which Sacrament is reserved

Monstrance veil
strip of white silk, without lining, with plain hemmed edges, nearly twice the height of monstrance

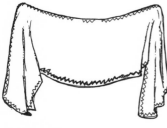

Humeral or offertory veil
(270 × 60 cm)
worn by priest when in procession or when moving the Sacrament; usually cream or white silk and lined

Tabernacle veils
in liturgical colours; divided in centre with hole for finial to protrude

Aumbry veil   *covers door of aumbry; sometimes embroidered*
Lenten veil   *covers statues during Lent*

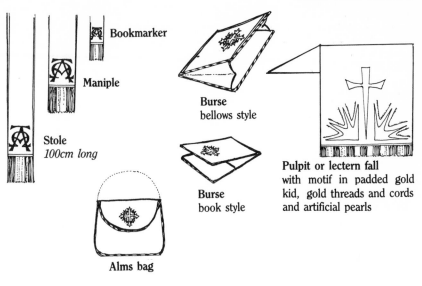

Bookmarker

Maniple

Stole
100cm long

Burse
bellows style

Burse
book style

Alms bag

Pulpit or lectern fall
with motif in padded gold
kid, gold threads and cords
and artificial pearls

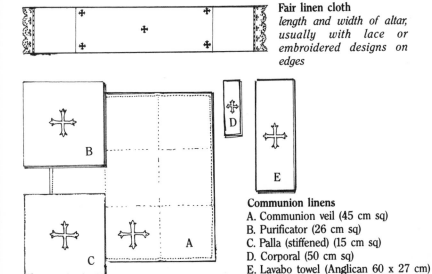

Fair linen cloth
length and width of altar,
usually with lace or
embroidered designs on
edges

Communion linens
A. Communion veil (45 cm sq)
B. Purificator (26 cm sq)
C. Palla (stiffened) (15 cm sq)
D. Corporal (50 cm sq)
E. Lavabo towel (Anglican 60 x 27 cm)
   (Roman catholic 50 x 40 cm)

Communion cloth
small white linen napkin to catch crumbs

Houselling cloth
white linen, the length of the altar rails

TEXTILES
Pads and Kneelers

Kneelers or **hassocks** protect worshippers from discomfort while kneeling. Cushions will be found at the altar, on the credence, in the pulpit and the sanctuary chair. Long padded **runners** will be used at the altar rail for kneeling worshippers or on benches for the seated congregation.

Pair of pale blue velvet wedding kneelers
on each a white silk satin-stitch embroidered
dove picked out in black tent stitch

Kneeler with crossed keys embroidered in gold silk petit-point against a shaded grey wool gros-point field. Side edges covered completely with red wool cross stitch.

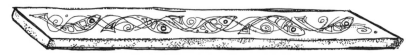

Bench runner with bold fish design and water effect in gold and silver kid leathers, cords and metallic threads. Emerald green velveteen sides.

Red velvet altar cushion with corded edges and long tassels attached to the corners by basket-stitch

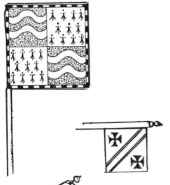

Knight's Banner square (90cm sq) bearing the owner's arms over the whole surface. Banners may also be rectangular.

In size they will conform to protocol: Princes' or Dukes' banners should be 123 cm sq; the King's banner should be 150 cm sq.

The banner commonly known as the *Royal Standard* is correctly *The Sovereign's Banner*

Banner roll small square

Standard either a long tapering flag split at the end, bearing the owner's device and motto (not arms or achievement) or an emblem on a staff

Pennant or pennon small pointed flag with two or more streamers, born at the lance head.

Gonfalon is similar but fixed to a bar. **Vexillium** scarf attached to a staff

Union Jack or Union Flag national ensign of the United Kingdom, combining the national banners of England, Scotland and Ireland, which may be flown on land by any British subject

Processional banner of the Mother's Union straight hung through loops

Figures of the Virgin and Child, in a combination of hand-worked applique and embroidery, against a pale blue ground. The name of the church at the top and the initials M U flanking the figures at the bottom. Blue and gold tasselled fringe.

Colour	infantry regimental flag
Colours	pair of infantry regimental flags
Other banners	might show St George; arms of the see or parish; the arms of a guild or society connected with the parish

TEXTILES
Rugs and Carpets

Carpets will be found on floors or as coverings for tables and benches.

A carpet over 100 years old is antique, over 60 years old is semi-antique and anything from 25 years ago can be regarded as old. The most famous carpets come from Persia and Afghanistan but, since the 15th century, Persian carpets have been copied by Spain, Poland (notable for European coats of arms), France (particularly tapestry carpets) and England, where they were copied in tent and cross stitch in the 16th and 17th centuries.

A fine carpet is judged by the quality of the wool; the tightness of the weave (in general the more knots per square inch, the better the quality); the shape and sheen; and the clarity and beauty of the design. The first step is to distinguish between pile, flat woven and embroidered carpets, then to recognise the 7 main oriental carpet-producing areas, before attempting to identify the individual types within the areas.

CARPET TYPES

Afghanistan	wine-red field with large octagon patterns
Caucasian	mosaic-like square or geometric designs enclosed in multicoloured diagonal bands; dragons; soft rose colour relieved by dark blue or black; ghiordes knot
Chinese	predominance of yellow; dragon, phoenix, lion, bat, cloud, swastika, pomegranate motifs (modern Chinese often made in Japan)
Indian	cotton; light pastel colours; French, Persian or Chinese style designs
Persian	repetitive all-over designs; central medallion, sometimes lobed or hung with festoons; decorated with pendants, lanterns and rectangular inscriptions; central motif often repeated at corners; gardens, hunting scenes and narratives (including Biblical narratives) popular; sehna and ghiordes knots
Turkish	small size; brilliant colours; borders with 7 ribbons decorated with flowers; geometric patterns; representations of Islamic mosque arch; no picture narratives; little green
Turkoman	deep glowing red; geometric patterns with wavy brown outlines; repetitive octagons and hexagons divided in various ways, sometimes cross-wise into 4 parts arranged in parallel and perpendicular rows, known as guls (flowers) or elephant's foot

PERSIAN SUB-TYPES

Feraghan	rusty background; palmettes and vegetation; Herati pattern; thin; green borders
Hamadan	natural camelhair background; dark geometric medallions; tortoise motif; heavy; single knots
Herat	dark blue or purple red background; closed rosettes in elongated leaves, ribbon-pattern, scroll or diamond; rosette with 8 points; green borders; very rich wool; rectangular shape; ghiordes or sehna knot
Heriz	light background; well spaced geometric patterns
Isfahan	bright background; symmetrical design; finely woven; repeated motif of hand grasping a phoenix; round medallion with 8 or 16 points
Kashan	small flowers filling centre and borders; soft silky wool; no symbols; bouquets resembling peacock feathers
Tabriz	plain background; large central medallion, repeated and quartered at corners; four seasons pattern; hunting scenes; ghiordes or sehna knot

Sehna knot
pile thread twisted
round one warp

Ghiordes knot
pile thread twisted
around two warps

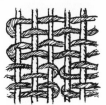

Kelim
threads incorporated
into weaving so that
rug can be used on
either side

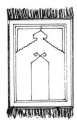

Mihrab design

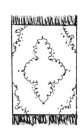

Medallion design

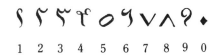

1 2 3 4 5 6 7 8 9 0

To calculate an equivalent Christian date,
subtract 1/33 from the Muslim date and
add 622 1428-1428 + 622 = 1990 33

$$1428 - \frac{1428}{33} + 622 = 1990$$

TEXTILES
Rugs and Carpets
CARPET MOTIFS

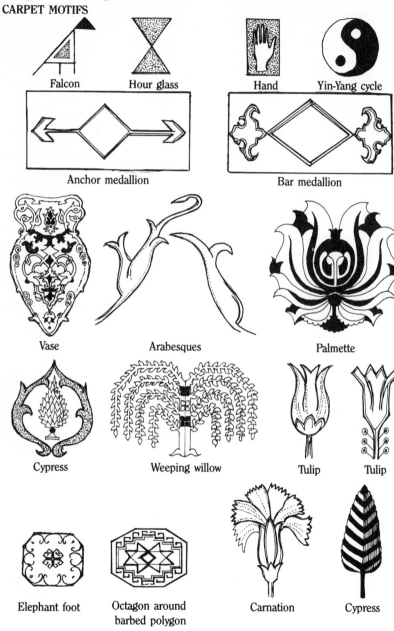

Falcon   Hour glass   Hand   Yin-Yang cycle

Anchor medallion   Bar medallion

Vase   Arabesques   Palmette

Cypress   Weeping willow   Tulip   Tulip

Elephant foot   Octagon around barbed polygon   Carnation   Cypress

Running dog

Crenellated

Recumbent S

Recumbent S

tchi or Cloud ribbon

Herati or Feraghan pattern

Tortoise

Tortoise

Mir

Mir
also called Pear or Cone

Star of Solomon

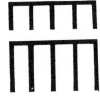

Combs

Fish or acanthus leaf

Water jug

Dagger

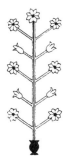

Tree of life

WOOD
Terms

One of the most common materials employed in churches, wood is chiefly used for furniture, either fixed or free standing. Until about 1550 most furniture was made from oak. In the 16th century walnut and exotic fruitwood inlays became popular along with beech, pine and cane. The end of the 17th century saw the development of gesso and lacquering techniques and mulberry and yew became more common. In the mid-18th century, the apogee of English furniture making, satinwood and imported mahogany finally replaced oak in fine furniture.

WOODS

Ash	light brown with yellowish streaky grain
Beech	pale, with satiny grain prone to woodworm, sometimes stained to resemble walnut. Used for heavy country furniture.
Chestnut	almost indistinguishable from oak
Elm	brown and tough, often used for seats
Mahogany	dark, with slight grain. Unknown before 1730
Mulberry	yellowish brown heavy tough wood with dark streaks. Used in veneers
Oak	heavy hardwood which darkens with age
Pine	yellow to red softwood. In use from 1660 and common in churches
Teak	light or dark brown, heavy and durable. In use in 20th century
Walnut	honey coloured (aged English wood) or darker red-brown (French and Italian) with tendency to woodworm. In use since 16th century
Yew	reddish to golden brown, very hard. Popular for country furniture

CONSTRUCTION TECHNIQUES

Mediaeval furniture was held together by mortice and tenon joints pinned with oak pegs or pins and with moulding cut into the solid joints. From the mid-16th century, applied mouldings and mitred corners began to appear although pinned and pegged mortice and tenon joints were still used. From the early 18th century joints were no longer pegged or pinned but, with an increasing emphasis on quality of finish, the use of dovetailing was most common.

Mouldings in 18th century furniture are generally applied and mitred.

Arris	sharp edge where two planes meet
Dovetailed	fan-shaped projections interlaced to form tight flat joint
Dowelled	spiked projection fitted into mortice to make tight joint
Joined construction	based on use of mortice and tenon joint
Mitre	diagonal joint formed by 2 mouldings
Mortice	cavity sunk in to receive projection (tenon) on another piece of wood
Tenon	projection protruded into cavity in another piece of wood
Boarded construction	planks held in place by nails or pegged with oak pins at the angles and strengthened with crosspieces

DECORATIVE TECHNIQUES

Applied	one piece of wood cut and applied to the surface of another
Carving	wood cut or gouged out to leave shapes, which may be freestanding, in relief or pierced as tracery
Cock beading	small astragal or bead moulding applied to edges of drawer fronts
Dado	wooden rail at height of chair backs or panelling on lower half of wall
Incising	cut or scratched into surface
Inlay	design cut from thin veneers of other woods and fitted into prepared cavities in the surface
Marquetry	complicated inlay designs, first fashionable in Holland and France
Mouldings	bands of wood of various shapes with name of architectural origin
Parquetry	geometric patterns inlaid or glued together to form a composite veneer
Pedestal	supporting base for statue, object etc rising to height of dado
Skirting	horizontal base board around bottom of wall
Stringing	inlay of thin lines of wood or bone
Veneer	thin sheet of richly figured (grained) wood, ivory or tortoiseshell glued or fitted into the surface of another

WOOD

WOOD
Terms

Baldacchino
*canopy over
altar, throne
or doorway*

Bracket
*decorative or functional
support for object*

Console
*any bracket or corbel of
scrolled form*

Console
*desk-like frame of
organ, containing
keyboards, stops etc*

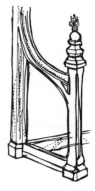

Bracket
pierced and pinnacled in
the form of a flying
buttress

Console mirror
*mirror supported by
bracket against wall*

Console table
*table supported by
bracket against wall*

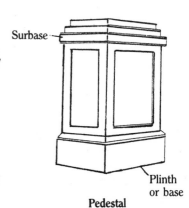

Surbase

Plinth
or base

Pedestal

162

Claw and ball   Hoof   Paw or hair claw   Pad

Ball   Bun   Turnip   Club

Spade   Marlborough   Stump   Stump

Knurl, spanish   Scroll   Gutta   Peg
or caterpillar

18th century bracket   Splayed bracket   Ogee bracket   Cabriole bracket

WOOD
Legs

16th century
cup and cover

17th century
cup and co

Columnar c.1620

Fluted c.1630

Bobbin turned
c.1660

Square moulded
c.1665

Ball turned
c.1670

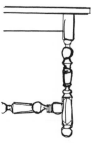

Columnar c.1670

Egg and disc
c.1670

Barley twist or spiral-
turned c.1670

Double scroll or
inverted c.1685

Umbrella c.1690

Turned tapered
c. 1690

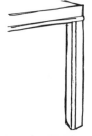

Square chamfered
(inside) from 1740

18th century
cabriole

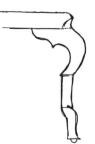

18th century broken
cabriole

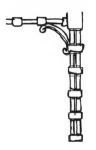

Cluster column or grouped pillar c.1760

Carved or applied fret c.1765

Square tapered c.1775

18th century hipped cabriole

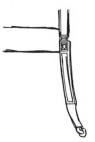

Late 17th century fluted vase stem

Pierced fret c. 1790

Reeded columnar c.1803

Sabre c.1815

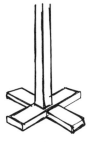

Vase-shaped slab standard or trestle

Cruciform

Tripod foot on stem

Splayed, split and wedged through seat

WOOD
Stretchers

Arched stretcher

Box stretchers

Cowhorn, spur, crinoline or hooped stretcher

Flat and serpentine cross stretcher

Shaped and joined by turned crossbar

Flat incurved stretcher

Floor level stretchers

H-stretcher

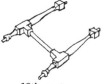

Rounded H-stretcher centred on baluster

Double H-stretcher with sausage turnings

18th century H stretcher

X-stretcher

X-stretcher Scrolled

X-stretcher Scrolled

Curved vertical X-stretcher

Curved horizontal X-stretcher

Wavy

PANELS

Wood panels are sometimes bevelled or rebated so as to create a border. **Wainscott** or **wainscotting** is generally used for wood panelling on walls or quarter sawn oak with rich figuring.

Styles of panelling have been copied in different periods

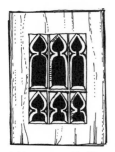

15th century Gothic
(pierced)

15th and 16th centuries
Gothic (pierced)

Early 16th century
Parchment

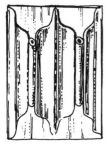

Early 16th century
Linenfold

Romayne
c.1530-1550

Mid-16th century
Renaissance

From 18th century
Fielded *(raised)*

From 18th century
Reticulated (pierced)

19th and 20th
centuries
Applied gothic tracery

WOOD

WOOD
Furniture

ALTAR AND COMMUNION RAIL

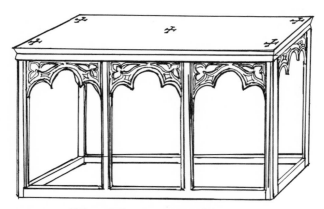

19th or 20th century purpose built altar

Rectangular frame with plain overhanging altar top incised with 5 consecration crosses
Front divided into 3 bays, back open, sides and each bay topped with flat arched pierced tracery panels with 2 cusps below and spandrel panels following shape of trefoil tracery
Framework members chamfered on outside and standing on base of rails (front and side panels often decorated with applied gothic tracery)

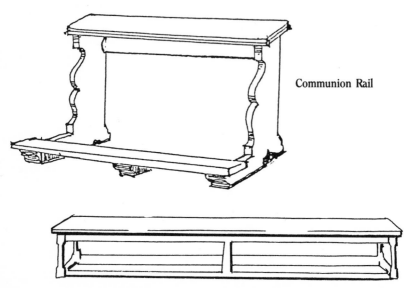

Communion Rail

Houselling Bench used as communion rail in some churches

BENCHES AND PEWS

Benches are seats with supports whereas **pews** are enclosed or elevated seating. The backs of benches usually have open rails or panels and will often have **bookrests** fitted to them for the use of the occupants of the bench behind. If the bookrests have flat surfaces they may date from before the Reformation for post-Reformation bookrests are usually sloping. Each section of benches will probably include a bench front or desk. Bench ends are often decorated with carving and finials known as **poppyheads**.

Pews have panels, doors and benches and may be raised above the floor or canopied or furnished and heated. Some are painted or carved with the names or coats of arms of families. The most popular material was oak until the 19th century when pine examples also appeared.

Stalls are individual or multiple seats placed against or returned against *(at right angles)* a wall or screen. Some have tabernacled canopies or traceried backs and cornices and nearly all have shaped side-panelling sometimes with carved or applied elbows. The stall fronts (or desks) may be traceried and have poppyheads. Stalls usually have tip-up seats known as **misericords**, which may be ornately carved on the underside. Subsidiary carvings on either side of the main projection are known as **supporters**.

Bench with close boarded back, moulded top rail and curved seat
Carved rectangular bench end
Unicorn below arch supporting pomegranate with branches flowing from top of stem to top of arch
Plain blind arcade below

Bench front with integral kneeler and level bookrest
Rectangular arch topped end with lively 16th century carving incorporating 2 quatrefoils below pelican in its piety and foliated poppyhead
Colonnade of round headed lancets single cusp each side between top and bottom rails, pierced triangular spandrels between arches

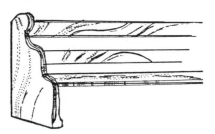

Open backed bench with two rails and one shaped end with simply moulded edging and one flush with wall

WOOD
Furniture

Stalls of 4 bays with a canopy formed of a cusped ogee arch over each stall, decorated with flame-like crockets and fleur-de-lys finials and supported by moulded shafts from shoulder rail
Moulded scrolled elbows
Misericord carved on the underside with green man

Early 17th century Box Pews

18th century Box Pews

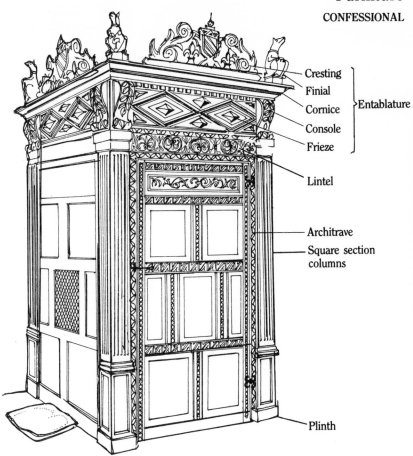

Cresting
Finial
Cornice ⎫ Entablature
Console
Frieze ⎭

Lintel

Architrave
Square section
columns

Plinth

Confessional

Confessional (possibly adapted from Elizabethan internal porch) of square frame and
panel construction of armoire style with reeded square columns on recessed panelled plinth
Talbot corner finials squatting on square plinths and holding shields between paws flanking
crestings of coats of arms amidst floriated scrolls and fleurs-de-lys
Large palmette carving on lintel and console brackets supporting cornice carved with leaves
Frieze enriched with applied mitred lozenge moulding surmounted by dentil moulding on
facade
Rails of door carved with geometric lined motif, muntins and stiles with guilloche, architrave
with irregular chevrons
Horizontal top panel carved with foliated scrolling tied at centre
Fielded panels plain
No architectural enrichment on sides other than fielded panels below the frieze and consoles
Metal grille set in panel at kneeling person's eye level on R side

WOOD
Furniture
BOXES

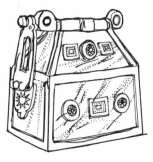

Feretory *container for saint's relics*
Metal rod across roofed top securing hasp with eyelets for attaching priest's neck cord
Pierced round and rectangular apertures in roof and sides

16th century oak alms box
Rectangular with rounded lid bound with iron straps and decorated with enamel tracery

17th century oak alms box
Rectangular with carved date and inscription on front
1684 REMEMBER THE PORE in arabic numerals and contemporary lettering supported on leaf bracket

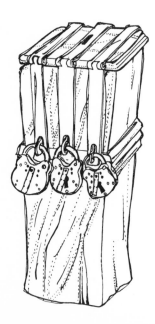

17th century poor box
Formed from hollowed oak post
Lid with coin slot has 3 iron straps hinged at front and secured to post by padlocks
Simple applied moulding around 3 sides as annulet

WOOD

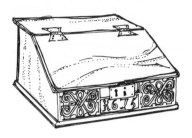

17th century desk-type oak bible box
Flat top, sloping flap and butterfly hinges on typical Lake District style interlace carving on front flanking keyplate above date 1675 in arabic numerals
Neatly moulded edges
Document drawers *(upright drawers)* within

17th century rectangular bible box with original lock and hasp with 2 large lunettes carved on front enclosing stylised leaf decoration and similar motifs in spandrels

20th century Book of Remembrance stand
Desk top with glazed viewing panel, supported on metal frame of pair of standards united by 2 stretchers and fixed to rear base of desk with feet curving forward to take balance

20th century Book of Remembrance stand in gothic style
Table style box with glazed top above carved frieze of running vine leaf ornament
Rectangular tracery panels of reticulated tracery running between legs on all 4 sides immediately below frieze and with blank shield at centre front

WOOD
Furniture
CHESTS

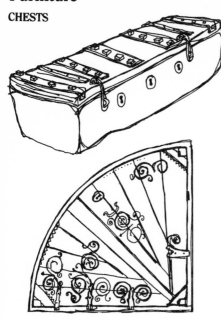

Mediaeval dugout
Hollowed log with solid slab lid,
strengthened by iron bands and strap
hinges with provision for 3 locks and
padlock loops

13th century cope chest
Quadrant shaped with frame of stout posts
at corners into which rails are tenoned
Lid in 2 halves with ornate scrolled and
foliated hinges and decoration
Panels of sides nailed into rebates in frame

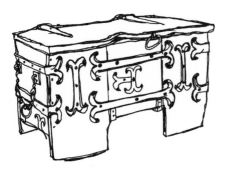

Early 14th century chest
Front and back tenoned into wide stiles
extended to provide legs
Iron straps binding chest with bifurcated
decorative ends
Chains with suspended rings at sides

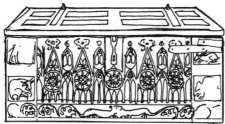

Flanders chest *(chest with traceried front)*
1550 to 1600
Front of 2 wide vertical stiles and 2 wide
horizontal planks
Traces of painted decoration in fantastic
bestiary scenes carved on stiles

WOOD

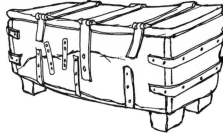

14th to 16th century chest
Massive planks pegged into corner posts of square section raising chest from floor strengthened by angled iron straps and flat straps (which strengthen the breaks in the timber)
Strap hinges continuing across top hinged to hasps and locks

15th century coffer for valuables
Tapering towards back and base, bound in grid of straight and scrolled straps with incised designs
Lid wider at top and pierced with coin slots, pivoting on 3 hinges
Large handles at each end

16th century counter
Chest with long legs about table height
Top scored

Early 17th century hutch
Top sawn and hinged for access
Frame and panel construction with 5 panels at front and back and 2 on sides decorated with linenfold with arrises gouged in series of V-shaped cuts
2 stretchers across length
Original doors fastened to frame

WOOD
Furniture

Early 17th century dole cupboard
Stamped enrichment on cornice
Geometric inlay on frieze
2 doors, each with 6 turned spindles in 2 stages
Pilasters carved with stiff leaves

17th century mule chest
Shallow type of panelled chest with drawers in lower part

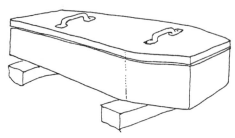

18th century mortsafe (earlier mortsafes usually lidless and of stone)

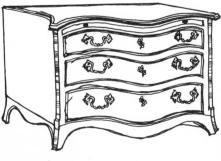

Late 18th century mahogany chest of drawers
Serpentine-fronted chest with oversailing top and cross banded canted corners, 3 long drawers with cockbeading, swan-necked rococo brass handles and C-scrolled escutcheons
Slide above top drawer
Splayed feet with bow-shaped apron on front and sides

Mid-19th century walnut davenport
Scrolled front uprights supporting scrolled
flap 4 drawers on L side and cupboard
door concealing 3 drawers on R side
Ink drawer on L
Bun feet

19th century military chest
2 staged flat sided chest with brass corners
and sunken handles, usually mahogany
(upper stage sometimes a secretaire)

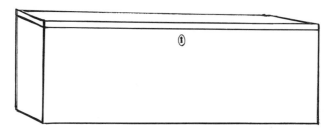

19th and 20th century deal frontal chest
Hinged top opening to enable frontal to
be hung on rods 105 cm x 300 cm x 30 cm

**19th and 20th century deal linen
and vestment press**

WOOD

WOOD
Furniture

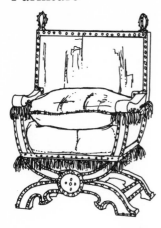

CHAIRS

The rake of the back, the shape of the arms, size, date, decoration and the construction material will vary from the chair types illustrated.

Chair of state c.1600

Armchair of horizontal X-frame construction, closely covered in crimson velvet, trimmed with fringed gold gallon and garnished with gilt headed nails and fitted with down stuffed cushion covered en suite

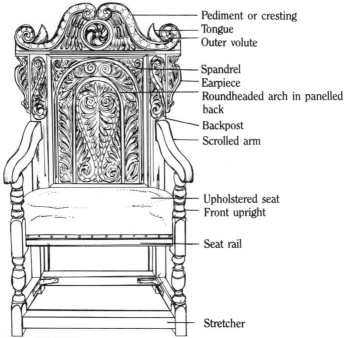

Pediment or cresting
Tongue
Outer volute

Spandrel
Earpiece
Roundheaded arch in panelled back
Backpost
Scrolled arm

Upholstered seat
Front upright

Seat rail

Stretcher

Yorkshire chair 1625-1650

Panel back construction, sometimes raked, panel carved with roundheaded arch decorated with scrolled foliage
Scrolled pediment with tongues protruding beside outer volutes carved with foliage and central roundel
Carving similar to back on ear pieces and back posts above scrolled arms
Turned front uprights of baluster form
Seat upholstered in red figured velvet with various reinforcements
Plain renewed stretcher

WOOD
Furniture

Glastonbury chair c.1630
(style copied in 19th century)
Chair with panel back and X-shaped legs
joined by crossbar and shaped arms from
seat to back, both held by wooden pins

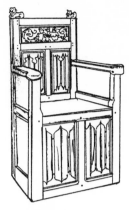

**Oak box
Cambridgeshire armchair
c.1530**
Square back surmounted
at either end by
crouching lion with
oblong panel of finely
carved Renaissance design
consisting of male and
female terminal figures
supporting trophy of arms
with tails ending in
scrolls, above 2
rectangular linenfold
panels
Flat arms enclosed with
plain panels
Back fitted behind with
cupboard door
2 linenfold panels in front
of box of simpler design
than back

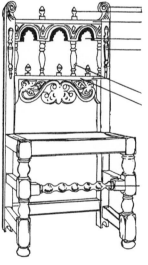

Finials
Upper rail of back
Arcaded back
Applied split
   balusters on
   backposts

Baluster columns
Lower rail of back

Mid-17th century Yorkshire or Derbyshire chair
Arcaded back; upper rail with 2 knob finials and 3 arches carved and incised decoration
and cusping supported by 2 baluster columns resting on lower rail with leafy scrolls and
3 knob finials
Crozier-shaped finials and applied split baluster ornaments to back uprights
Spirally turned front rail stretcher; other stretchers plain
New feet on front legs; castor slots cut on back legs
Seat sunk for squab cushion

WOOD

WOOD
Furniture

Early 17th century
Jacobean oak settle
Top rail of back treated with lunettes
Lozenge carving in 4 panelled back

Lancashire panel back chair c. 1660
Flat pyramidal caps to backposts
Lunette cresting carved with tulip amidst
sprawling foliage above similar carving
with dog-rose on rectangular panel
Opening below panel
Grooved seat rails
Turned front legs
Bobbin-turned front rail stretcher

Walnut armchair c.1670
Elaborately carved cresting of back and rail joining front
cabriole legs in openwork with putti crowning female
figure, flanked by putti blowing trumpet
Spiral uprights with crowned female head finials
Lion couchant on each armrest
Side of back adorned with openwork carvings of putti
amidst vines and roses growing from baskets
Original canework back; seat (formerly caned)
upholstered in green velvet

Beech chair c.1690

Tall back with moulded arched cresting rail, with ears and straight lower back rail enclosing 5 vertical moulded spars

Front seat rail with veneered and shaped apron, hidden by fringe of red

Victorian plush covering slightly tapered seat

Turned front legs with ball feet, united by turned front stretcher rail

Turned H-stretchers uniting all 4 legs with slight splaying on back legs

Carefully mitred mouldings at corners where back uprights join cresting rail

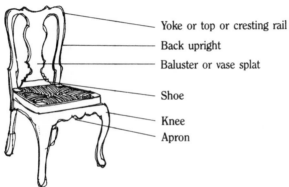

Yoke or top or cresting rail

Back upright

Baluster or vase splat

Shoe

Knee

Apron

Early 18th century side chair

Shaped back and serpentine cresting rail; cabriole front legs with pad feet; wavy apron; rush seat and no underframing

Mid 19th century hall chair
Cast iron frame and elm seat
Back of facing S scrolls with fragmentary label attached
behind (probably from auction catalogue) attributing
chair to hall at Fawley Castle
Heavily grooved seat rails resting on pair of acanthus
ornamented tied X scrolls united by grooved bar

19th and 20th century church chair
Beech frame and elm or rush seat
Top rail usually shaped and middle rails bowed
Book pocket between backposts
Box stretcher with attached shelf for kneeler
Often made in Buckinghamshire

COUNTRY STYLE CHAIRS

Windsor chairs

The most popular country chair design of the 19th century is very distinctive and often found in churches. Windsor chairs come in many shapes but usually have elm seats, beech spindles (struts, stays or rods) beech legs and stretchers and ash in the bowed parts.
The legs and supports are pegged into the seat and the legs invariably splayed. In some examples, two stays form a brace from the top of the back to a bobtail projecting from the rear of the seat. A horizontal hoop forms a semi-circle across the back and long the front as arm supports. Every variant of style has a name, for example, if the hooped back at arm level is missing, the chair is a **single hooped windsor.**

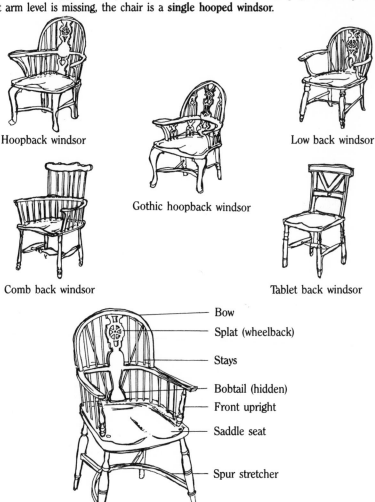

Hoopback windsor

Gothic hoopback windsor

Low back windsor

Comb back windsor

Tablet back windsor

Bow

Splat (wheelback)

Stays

Bobtail (hidden)

Front upright

Saddle seat

Spur stretcher

WOOD
Furniture

18th century Yew
gothic windsor armchair
Arch bow
Ash saddle seat
Cabriole legs
Club feet
Crinoline (spur) stretcher and turned back
supports

19th century
Mendlesham windsor armchair
Low back with double cresting rails of
square section infilled with 3 upturned
balls
Flat outward curving arms extending
beyond sloping supports
Saddle seat splayed legs and H-stretcher

Smoker's bow windsor c.1860

Lath back windsor

High back ladderback

CHAIRBACKS

Queen Anne

Fiddle

Lyre

Shield

Square

Gothick

Late 18th century
Oval

19th century
Balloon

Ribband

Ladder

Prince of Wales
feathers

WOOD
Furniture

19th century
Shouldered balloon

19th century
Spoon hall seat

19th century gothic

19th century
Elizabethan

DOORS

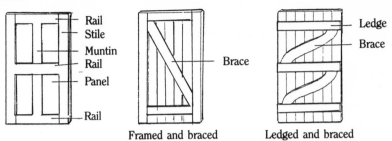

Rail
Stile
Muntin
Rail
Panel

Rail

Brace

Framed and braced

Ledge
Brace

Ledged and braced

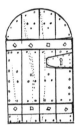

Saxon door with ledges on rear

Saxon and early mediaeval doors were stout defences made of thick oak boards placed vertically on the outside and horizontally inside for added strength. The toolmarks are still visible and the doors were fastened together by long wrought-iron nails with ornamental heads, driven through the door and clenched on the inside. Ledges were always confined to the back of the door.

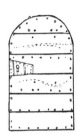

Norman door with alternating horizontal hinges with double scrolled bifurcated terminals

In the 12th century, although construction techniques were similar, doors were often decorated by the smith with wrought iron hinges, locks, handles and knockers. The hinges usually have bifurcated ends and stamped work of contemporary design.

The smith declined in prominence in the 14th century and decoration on doors came into the realm of the carpenter. Locks and hinges were therefore plainer but tracery was carved into the woodwork or moulding applied with glue and nails.

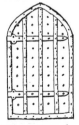

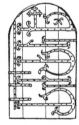

14th century door   **14th century door**

In the late 17th century the smith's craft enjoyed a slight revival and decorated hinges reappear.

The majority of churches have 19th century doors, often exact copies of earlier Norman doors but the decoration on the later doors tends to be more precise.

WOOD
Furniture

FONT COVERS

In the mediaeval period, wooden font covers (often highly decorative) were fitted to fonts to protect the holy water. Mediaeval font covers were copied in the 19th century as part of the gothic revival movement.

Cone font cover
Lightly moulded octagonal base with moulded ribs, each with 3 crockets rising from each corner to neck surmounted by 4 tiered finial
Flat panels enclosed by ribs

Crown font cover
Simple octagonal flat cover supporting 8 ogee scrolls, unmoulded but with carved rosettes on both sides of the volute of each scroll
Central junction terminated in bulb finial with turned baluster rising from cover to intersection of scrolls

3 staged tabernaclework font cover
Pinnacled and spired in receding tiers incorporating telescopic device for lifting by **font crane**
Lofty crocketed pinnacle with gables at base and finial top supported on 5 slender annulated columns
Cruciform in plan with 4 slender annulated compound columns at centre with roofs projecting on 4 sides supported by slender annulated column at each corner
Crocketed gable with centre pinnacle on outside face of each roof
Square in plan with 4 intersecting roofs with crocketed gable ends with finials and pierced trefoil in gable end above arch
Arch on each face, moulded and decorated with ball flowers, filling most of gable, supported on slender annulated columns with stand on base filled by panel of blind tracery consisting principally of 2 quatrefoils
Similar column in centre of arch supporting open tracery filling arch
Arched head with two cusps and centre pointed foil supporting circlet with trefoil in each light
Caps to columns but no bases
Centre structure supported by flying buttresses set on diagonal and containing polychromed figure of Christ kneeling and John the Baptist standing
Base with band of moulding formed from geometrical pattern of mostly circular indentations with band of fishscale decoration inclined inwards

PULPITS AND DESKS

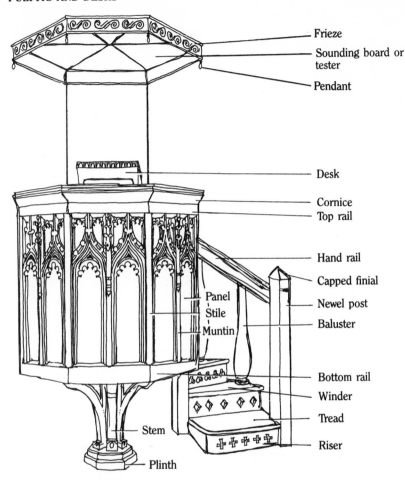

Frieze

Sounding board or tester

Pendant

Desk

Cornice
Top rail

Hand rail

Capped finial

Newel post

Baluster

Panel
Stile
Muntin

Bottom rail

Winder

Tread

Riser

Stem

Plinth

15th century oak pulpit
Octagonal **drum** with panels on 6 facets subdivided by centre muntin with buttress and pinnacle springing at mid-point, richly decorated with deeply moulded ogee arch with crocketed top edge but no finial and internal arches with round heads with cinquefoil tracery and spandrel panels with trefoil tracery flanking ogee arches

Desk made from 15th or 16th century oak with carved edges
19th century stem with attached brackets on octagonal plinth
19th century octagonal **sounding board** with pendant finials at each angle and frieze of scrolled carving attached

19th century **stairway** of 4 threads on S side, each riser pierced with set of 5 crosses, lozenges, trefoils, quatrefoils in ascending order
Plain rectangular **newel post** with pyramidal capped finial, grooved hand rail and plain balusters

WOOD
Furniture

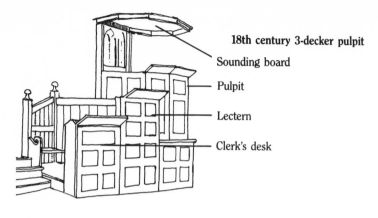

18th century 3-decker pulpit

Sounding board

Pulpit

Lectern

Clerk's desk

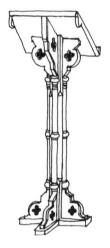

19th century oak lectern *(see METAL: Lecterns)*
Book rest supported on solid cruciform brackets with shaped and bevelled edges, each bracket pierced in centre with quatrefoil

Stem of clustered shafts with annulets attached to rectangular central shaft

Cruciform base with plain sill and supporting brackets pierced in centre with quatrefoil

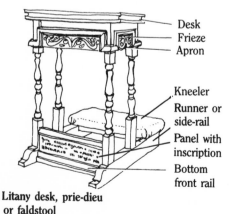

Desk
Frieze
Apron

Kneeler
Runner or
side-rail
Panel with
inscription
Bottom
front rail

**Litany desk, prie-dieu
or faldstool**

Credence

RAILS
Moulded top rail
Wrought iron columnar supports (or standards) rising from octagonal buttressed bases with spiral-twist centre sections between knots and ivy decorated brackets splaying either side of upper part
Integral kneeler formed by oak sill

Moulded top rail with incised lunettes on frieze
Pillar-turned baluster between sturdier standards of the same shape which have cup and cover finials
Grooved and domed bottom rail tenoned into bases of standards, balusters and rail

17th or 18th century Laudian *(enclosing altar)* **communion rail**

Gallery (or tribune) with balustrade consisting of groups of five turned balusters separated by fluted stiles
Scrolled frieze above lower cornice

WOOD
Furniture

SCREENS

Screens, particularly that which divided the chancel from the centre of the church, were an essential part of mediaeval religious practice. The congregational principles of the Reformation led to the wholesale destruction of chancel screens which were not generally reintroduced until the 19th century. Screens were also used, however, to separate side chapels and other areas of the church.

On **rood screens**, the Rood figures are usually placed centrally with the cross rising from a tall pedestal and the flanking figures on small pedestals. Original groups are very rare, though a few survive in Wales, and most date from the religious revival of the 1840's. Many were polychromed and a torch or magnifying glass often reveals traces of original colour in the corners and recesses. Where the chancel arch was boarded in above the rood screen, the resultant tympanum was sometimes painted with a Doom scene showing the division of souls into Heaven and Hell.

Screens are usually divided into a series of bays with an opening which may or may not be gated. The outer bays are generally panelled at the base and open, except for ornament, between the **transom** *(centre)* rail and the **head** *(top)* rail. The heads of the **lights** *(openings)* usually have pierced carved tracery.

Bressumer beam	horizontal beam supporting main superstructure
Ceilure	section of roof directly above rood screen, sometimes richly decorated as canopy to the rood
Chancel screen	dividing chancel from nave
Chantry screen	dividing tomb chapel from chancel or nave
Parclose screen	separating chapel from body of church
Quire screen or pulpitum	dividing eastern section of cruciform church from body of church (opposite rood screen)
Rood beam	beam spanning chancel arch supporting rood *(Christ on the Cross)*
Rood screen	screen incorporating Christ on the Cross invariably flanked by figures of Mary (right) and St John (left)
Roodloft	space above vaulted or coved rood screen which supports gallery fronts at east and west sides
Tower screen	separating tower from nave

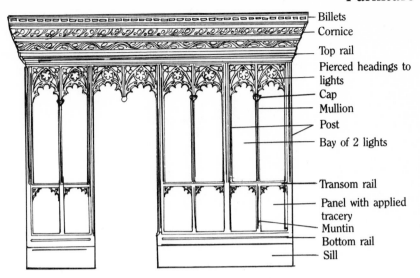

Billets
Cornice
Top rail
Pierced headings to lights
Cap
Mullion
Post
Bay of 2 lights

Transom rail
Panel with applied tracery
Muntin
Bottom rail
Sill

Screen with 4 bays and opening in 2nd bay from N end
Main frame heavily moulded standing on plain chamfered sill
Cornice with billets above 2 rows of running ornaments (wide twisted stem with foliage in alternating twists and running vine trail) contained by beads and fillets
Slender moulded mullion with ball shaped cap but no base extends from transom to top rail
Shallow arched head to each light with cinquefoil tracery and another arch springing from same point rising to top of light
Circlet with cinquefoil between two arches
Trefoil following shape of light with foliated boss linking cusps in flanking spandrels
2 plain panels below transom rail in each by divided by centre muntin with triangular tracery panels applied in each corner consisting of 2 cusps and pocket in spandrel

Vaulted rood screen with 5 bays, central doors and gallery front on W side

Central Cross on tall octagonal pedestal with cap and base and carved ornamented ends to arms and pierced tracery at central intersection INRI on label above head of traditionally carved Christus

Figures of Mary *(sorrowful expression and downcast eyes)* and John *(head upturned towards Christ)* on octagonal pedestals with caps and bases, both with hands clasped in prayer. Gallery with 10 full panels and 2 half panels divided by moulded posts with bases

Cornice with single row of running ornament above cinquefoil tracery at head of each panel

Cornice with 2 rows of ornament (flowing foliage over deep hollow paterae) spaced over each post and arch

Main posts supporting vaulted loft fully moulded with caps and bases

Centre mullion (without cap or base) in each bay above transom rail dividing space into 2 lights, each with arched head with cinquefoil tracery

Concave rib springing from top of each arch joins its pair in centre of main arch enclosing space cusped to form quatrefoil

Beneath transom rail, centre muntin divides each bay into 2 panels, each divided by further muntin into lancets with tracery heads with 2 cusps and centred circular foil

Concave rib springing from lancet head to join its pair at top of panel

Centre bay wider than side bays with pair of doors to height to transom rail, each with full panel as side bays and stiles which meet and rise above transom rail to form finial

STOOLS

Chairs developed from more simple stool shapes but never completely supplanted stools. Early inventories distinguish between highstools, lowstools, foot stools and elbow *(arm)* or back *(side)* chairs. The mediaeval backstool, in use until the late 18th century, is the hybrid with most in common with stools and chairs.

Backstool pre-1790

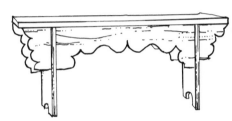

Oak form c.1520 of plank construction
Apron extending beyond solid supports to ends of seat of ogee shape with rounded ends
Supports with grooved edges and arched openings below

Joined stool from 1550
4 turned legs straddling outwards and united by rail beneath seat linked by floor level stretchers (19th century coffin stools are similar but with longer legs)

Early 17th century folding faldstool

Baroque stool with spanish feet c.1690
Arched scrolled central stretcher and 2 turned side stretchers with block central section

WOOD
Furniture

Tables

14th to 16th century oak trestle table
Plank top supported by trestles with ogee opening at base
Pair of central stretchers with protruding ends secured by wooden pegs

Elizabethan oak drawleaf table
c.1600 Moulded frieze with deeply carved diagonal gadroons 4 bulbous legs with cups carved with acanthus and nulled covers
Square section floor-level stretchers

Jacobean oak or elm table
c.1640 Top formed of 3 planks with apron 6 thin tapered turned legs joined by square section stretchers

17th century country oak side table
Inlaid banding of fruit wood let into solid oak around top and drawer
Wide apron rail of William and Mary style with cock-beading around edge
Neatly turned legs of baluster shape
Joints pegged
Barley twist H-stretchers

Oak side table c.1670
Frame of halved hexagonal shape with circular top folded in centre
Gate at rear with square section stretcher
6 turned baluster legs
Halved hexagonal bottom board possibly used as credence *(sanctuary table)*

Stuart dresser c. 1680

Gate-leg table from 1730

D-end table c.1780

Pembroke table c.1800

Sofa table c.1820

20th century trestle credence *(sanctuary table)*
Ogee-shaped apron carved with cursive lilies attached to moulded top-rail stretcher between plain pillar trestles with canted corners
Plain moulded domed bottom stretcher

WOOD
Small Wooden Objects

Beadle's mace   Constable's truncheons

Collection plate

Collection ladles

OBJECTS

CLOCKS
Terms

The clock in the tower (with or without an external dial) is known as a **turret or tower clock**. Vestries may contain a variety of domestic clocks, which may be broadly divided into two classes, **wall-hanging** and **free standing**. The commonest wall clock is the **dial clock**, spring driven and contained in a circular wooden case, occasionally with a downward extension to accommodate a longer pendulum. **Tavern** or **Act of Parliament clocks** have a long trunk section to accommodate weights and a long pendulum. **Lantern or hood clocks** may occasionally be found. Of free-standing clocks, the most usual are **mantel or bracket clocks**, which are spring driven and stand upon a mantel piece, or other horizontal surface. **Longcase or grandfather clocks** are less likely to be found in churches; these are weight driven and stand on the floor. In addition, some clocks are built into galleries or other parts of the structure. The maker's name will usually give a clue to the date but only if features of the clock and case support his dates.

Bob	weight at end of pendulum
Dial	clock face
Fret	pierced brass decoration on lantern clocks
Fusée	pulley to equalise weight of mainspring
Hood	top section of longcase clock which generally lifts off in pre-1690 clocks
Lenticle	glass let into door of longcase clocks to allow motion of bob to be seen; known as **bull's eye** when glazed with thick green glass; obsolete by 1710.
Movements	working parts of clock
Splat	decorative panel at top of clock
Tablet	decorative panel at bottom of clock (rare)
Weights	cylindrical lead, cast iron or brass sheeted weights hung from chains

Hooded clock with weights c. 1745

Fret

Lantern clock with weights c. 1680

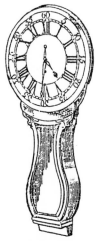

Act of Parliament clock, 1797 Weight-driven and unglazed

DIAL CLOCKS

Cases are ebonised or of common furniture woods, while some early 19th century ones have brass or mother of pearl inlay. Later examples of German or American clocks have fancy inlay bandings and usually having a downward extension with a glazed door showing the pendulum. Clocks with this extension are known as **drop dial clocks.**

Dials Early dials may be of silvered brass and some painted wooden specimens survive. The vast majority are made of painted iron, some convex but most flat. German and American clocks have dials of painted zinc.

Movements English movements have a fusée and only a few strike. German and American clocks have open springs, no fusées and usually strike.

LONGCASE CLOCKS

Cases are made of the same woods and have the same designs and mouldings as furniture, but mahogany is rare before 1750. In general later ones are taller and broader than early examples, but many cottage clocks follow smaller, simpler, early designs.

Dials 17th century dials are small and square, but later ones usually larger. Break-arch dials are normal from c. 1715, but many square dials continued to be made, especially for cottage clocks, which often had only one hand until 1800. Painted dials were introduced c. 1775 but did not entirely supplant engraved brass.

Movements 8-day and longer duration movements almost invariably rely on catgut, metal or nylon lines to support weights. 30 hour clocks usually have a single weight on an endless chain or rope.

CLOCKS

Dial clock
English c. 1850
Painted flat dial
Non-striking
Mahogany case

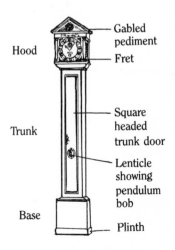

Hood

Trunk

Base

Gabled pediment

Fret

Square headed trunk door

Lenticle showing pendulum bob

Plinth

Late 17th century architectural longcase case clock with square dial

CLOCKS
Types

BRACKET OR
MANTEL CLOCKS

In the 18th century, most examples will be English, while in the 19th century French clocks are common while German and American copies of both occur in late 19th century.

Cases English examples use the same woods as longcases, French ones often have cast iron cases.

Dials English dials are smaller versions of longcase dials, normally without seconds; French dials are usually circular.

Movements English, French and the best German examples are good quality, American ones less so.

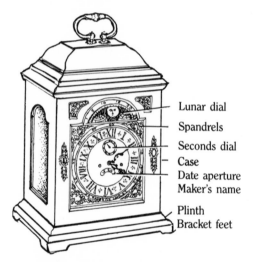

Lunar dial

Spandrels

Seconds dial

Case
Date aperture
Maker's name

Plinth
Bracket feet

18th century mahogany Mantel or Bracket clock
Arched ornamental dial showing phases of the moon, asymmetrical rococo spandrels, key escutcheon and matching blind escutcheon and corner pieces flanking the lunar dial.
Wavy minute hand.
Arabic minute figures, plain silvered chapter ring, seconds dial and large date aperture.
Maker's name at base of applied chapter ring.

Monuments inside churches range from large, elaborate canopied tombs to modest tablets affixed to the wall. They may be simple inscriptions or they may include sculpture, carving and elaborate decoration. Costumed figures, lettering, symbols, heraldry and architectural images all appear on monuments and memorials. Some were plain but early tombs may have been coloured. Sadly, it is rare for any original colour to have survived, but late 19th century restorers have sometimes attempted to return mediaeval monuments to the rich hues in which they first appeared.

Monuments are full of clues to the history of the church and its community. They can tell us about the people who lived around the church and what they looked like, how wealthy the community was and why, why and how people died in different periods and many other details of their lives. They are also full of information on contemporary artistic style, philosophy and religious observance.

In the mediaeval period, all tombs and memorials stood on the floor, either against the wall or away from it. Wall monuments, entirely supported on the wall, were virtually unknown before the 16th century. **Floor monuments** were either large carved tombs or simple floor slabs and generally either contained or lay over the mortal remains of the person or family they commemorate. **Wall monuments**, on the other hand, mostly consist of a tablet bearing an inscription in an architectural frame or cartouche and did not necessarily relate to where the body had been interred.

Over time, monuments tend to have been moved around the church and churchyard and may be nowhere near their original site.

- Achievement
- Pediment
- Cornice
- Shoulders
- Tablet with inscription
- Flanking pilasters
- Wings
- Apron with blank shield
- Brackets

Nowy-headed tablet

Rectangular tablet with arched head

MEMORIALS & MONUMENTS
Floor Slabs

Floor Slabs

Pre-1300

Slabs taper from head to foot and are usually of local materials but Purbeck marble was commonly used for quality work. In the 12th century, slabs are ornamented with a variety of designs, carved in low relief or incised, often a cross or symbol to indicate the profession of the deceased, but usually without lettering. From 1200, the slab might bear a representation of the deceased in stone or brass but not a likeness.

13th-17th centuries

Brasses, made of thin plates of copper/zinc alloy, were commonly set flush into the stone. Often only the indent of the brass survives today, the original having been lost or destroyed, but even a worn indent should give an idea of at least the shape of the brass.

17th and 18th centuries

Massive slabs of marble or bluish-grey stone were widely used, often with an achievement in bas-relief and an incised inscription in roman lettering.

19th century

The making of figured brass for monuments was revived as part of a general movement towards mediaeval revival but monuments of a wide variety of materials and styles are found.

 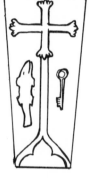  

| 12th or 13th century stone coffin lid with cross in relief | 13th century slab with incised fleurée cross and fish and key symbols | 14th century slab with indent of figure, panels and two shields | 17th century grey marble with bas-relief achievement in roundel above inscription |

Effigies

Before 1500, almost all tomb effigies are recumbent. The earliest effigies had legs and hands in various positions, but from the early 14th century arms are usually rigidly straight with hands together in prayer. Married couples may hold hands.

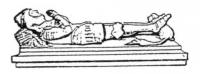

Effigies were rarely portraits of the dead.

Figures carved on tomb chests may help to date it. Weepers *(grieving members of the family, usually offspring)* occur from the late 13th century (1); angels from the late 14th century (2); and saints in the 15th century (3).

1   2   3

The heads of effigies may be supported by pillows or held by angels. A knight's head may rest on a helmet, his feet against a couchant lion or other beast. Small figures of bedesmen (4) may be found on a couchant lion's back and pieces of armour around the effigy.

4

Cadavers *(effigy of the deceased after death)* may occur alone or in addition to an effigy in life and serve as a memento mori.

MEMORIALS & MONUMENTS
Floor and Wall Monuments

1550 to early 17th century

Renaissance forms and decoration superseded gothic, characterised by the use of columns, obelisks, strapwork, ribbonwork, grotesques, cherub heads and allegorical figures. Tombs were frequently contained in pavilions or canopies. Effigy postures were stiff, recumbent, reclining or kneeling at prayer. Demi-figures appeared and, after 1600, sitting or standing figures. Roman lettering predominated, although gothic was still used in the provinces. Effigies were dressed in contemporary costume. Painted and gilded alabaster was very popular. **Notable sculptors:** *Maximilian Colt, Gerard and Nicholas Johnson, William and Cornelius Cure.*

Early to mid-17th century

The classical style was now more refined, especially with the use of pediments on architectural canopies and frames; white and black marble competed with alabaster as popular materials. Effigies, in contemporary dress, were found in a variety of poses and were generally less stiff with hands in various positions. Pedestal busts were introduced in this period. Sculptors' signatures were rare and are easily confused with the mark or name of the mason who erected the monument. **Notable sculptors:** *Epiphanius Evesham, Nicholas Stone, Edward and Joshua Marshall, the Christmas family.*

1660 to early 18th century

For the baroque tombs of this period, marble superseded alabaster. Recumbent and kneeling effigies were increasingly rare and relief medallion portraits appear. Costume was usually contemporary but figures may wear Roman armour. Allegorical figures, particularly the Virtues, were common as were symbols of mortality and immortality. **Notable sculptors:** *Grinling Gibbons, John Nost, Thomas Green, Caius Gabriel Cibber, John Bushnell, Francis Bird, William and Edward Stanton.*

Mid-18th century

Architectural canopies disappeared after c.1750. Black or grey marble as a two-dimensional pyramid background to standing wall monuments and the combined use of different coloured marbles on one monument were popular. Figures were often dressed as Romans, sometimes in armour, sometimes loosely wrapped in toga-like garments, standing or reclining on a sarcophagus or against an urn. Small portrait medallions, busts, putti, urns, cartouches and symbols of mortality or immortality abound. Decoration was rococo. **Notable sculptors:** *Louis Francis Roubillac, John Michael Rysbrack, Henry, Peter and Thomas Scheemakers, Henry Cheere, Joseph Wilton.*

Late 18th and early 19th centuries

A more restrained neo-classical style had developed, inspired by ancient Greece, particularly a stele design. Black and white marble were still popular, white increasingly so. Recumbent effigies began a gradual come-back but the most typical figure of this period was a mourning female leaning over an urn or sarcophagus. Angels were common, often receiving the deceased at death. Dress was stylised or contemporary but naval and military effigies were often in uniform. **Notable sculptors:** *Joseph Nollekens, John Bacon and his son, John, Thomas Banks, Richard Westmacott, John Flaxman, Francis Chantrey, John Francis Moore.*

Victorian period

The Greek revival continued, but the gothic style enjoyed a massive revival. Black and white marble were still common but alabaster revived as a popular material. Canopies survived but the period marked the return of tomb chests with recumbent effigies. Reclining seated and standing effigies were much rarer. Fashions in costume and lettering were eclectic. **Notable sculptors:** *Peter Hollins, Richard Westmacott the Younger, Joseph Boehm, Henry Armstead, Frederick Thrupp.*

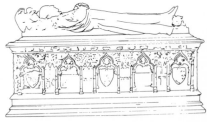

MEMORIALS & MONUMENTS
Tablets

17th century tablet
Putto on either side of urn
Pedestal bust set in oval niche
Cartouche inscription tablet

Mid- 18th century tablet
Closed urn
Panel carved in high relief,
Curved and angular apron

**Cartouche with scrolls,
flowers and drapery**

**Winged cherubs' heads
Achievement**

Late-19th century rectangular brass tablet with concave
corners. Incised and black inlaid cursive vine border.
Inscription, with flourished capitals, beginning and
ending with a rubricated patée cross.

Early 19th century symbolism:
opium poppies (the sleep of death);
sickle cutting rosebud (death taking child)

Stele
background

Lozenge tablet

Square tablet with
clipped, chamfered
or canted corners
on ground of
conforming shape

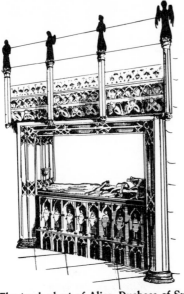

The tomb chest of Alice, Duchess of Suffolk, d. 1475.
Made of alabaster, it was probably erected soon after her death and stands between the chancel and St John's Chapel

The tomb chest stands under a horizontal canopy of panelled stone, with an elaborate cornice of tiers, the lowest formed of winged demi figures of angels, each with hand folded on the breast; alternate angels have a crown or tonsure and one has a cross on his forehead. Above the figures is a band of quatrefoils. The uppermost tier consists of elaborate quatrefoil cresting.

The canopy is divided vertically into 3 equal sections by stone shafts rising from foliated bosses and the capitals crowned with battlements on which stand carved wooden figures, 4 on each side

The actual tomb-chest also consists of three tiers. On top is the recumbent figure of the Duchess wearing widow's weeds over contemporary dress with a ducal coronet on her head, a ring on the third finger of the right hand and the Garter on the left forearm. Her hands are folded in prayer and her head rests on a cushion supported by 2 angels on each side. Above her head is an elaborate canopy carved from a single block of alabaster. At her feet is a lion. Above her feet, on the panelling, is a bracket presumably for the image of a saint

The sides of the tomb chest, on which the Duchess lies, is carved with a row of canopied niches occupied by frontally standing angels bearing shields with coats of arms. Brass fillets on the cornice of the tomb chest, on both north and south sides, carry the inscription in Black Lettered latin

Below the chest is an open space, enclosed by an arcade of 8 arches on either side, within which may be seen a cadaver clothed in a shroud. On the roof of this compartment, only to be seen by lying on the floor and looking through the arcades, are two frescoes, St Mary Magdalene and St John on one side and the Annunciation on the other, a copy of which may be seen on the chancel side of the entrance to the Chapel

The canopy, side panelling and lowest tier of the tomb are unpainted. The Duchess, and everything on her level, and the tomb chest are parcel gilt and painted.

Condition of the whole tomb chest is excellent.

MEMORIALS & MONUMENTS
Wall Tablet

Rectangular architecturally framed alabaster tablet in memory of Richard Hampden d. 1662 and his wife Ann d.1663

The cream alabaster tablet has a plain black marble border with an inscription incised in roman lettering, capitals and lower case.

The marble frame is flanked by white veined, free-standing, angled Ionic columns which support a moulded cornice and segmented pediment with black tympanum, against which and protruding above is a carved and painted achievement

Grey marble, acanthus scrolled, tapering wing brackets flank the tablet against the wall

The tablet and columns rest on a black marble shelf supported by black erect consoles with white marble architraves, between which, set against the wall, is a carved shield with painted coat of arms.

Sculptor's signature N.O.N.E. on right edge of shelf

Here lyeth § body of
RICHARD HAMPDEN
Cittizen of London
third son of
S͏ᵗ EDMVND HAMPDEN
of ABBINGDON in § COUNTY of
NORTHAMPTON. He departed
this life the nihth day of
September 1662

And also the body of
ANN
his wife the daughter of
FRANCIS LANE
Cittizen of London
She departed this life
the ninth day of
March 1663

Sarcophagus with putto sitting at either end of lid, one holding staff with cap of liberty, the other a scroll inscribed Magna Charta. In the centre of the lid is an acanthus spray with ribbands stretching to the putti

Directly above is an oval bas-relief with ribband cresting and moulded frame, depicting an oak tree hung with coloured shields of Hampdens and allied families, rising from a scene of Chalgrove battlefield (where the parliamentarian, John Hampden was slain in 1643)

On the front of the sarcophagus is an inscription in roman lettering, capitals and lower case, straight and slanting, relating to John Hampden d.1754 and his descent from John Hampden (above)

On the apron, between scrolled and acanthus decorated brackets and with an acanthus spray below the curved and angular lower edge, is the dedication in the same lettering. The condition is excellent. Only the shields are painted

18th century standing wall monument

Large standing wall monument to Henry Petty, 1st Earl of Shelburne and his family in Roman dress

The monument has a broad base with slightly projecting pedestal-like ends, bearing a large sarcophagus of grey marble, upon which reclines the effigy of the Earl in Roman tunic and toga, with the reclining figure of his wife holding an open book in her left hand.

The front of the sarcophagus bears a portrait medallion of Sir William Petty, the Earl's father and founder of the family

On each side of the monument there is a pair of composite unfluted columns supporting a broken triangular pediment, upon the apex of which is a garlanded urn. Upon one side reclines the figure of Justice and on the other, Truth. Below the feet of each is an urn.

Under arch of pediment is heraldic achievement carved in relief

Immediately below, against a tapering back panel swathed in drapery, are 2 putti among clouds holding a wreath over the head of the expired nobleman

Standing upon the pedestal on the dexter side stands the figure of the Earl's son James (died aged 40) dressed in Roman senatorial robes. By his side sits his wife (died aged 32) with their son on her lap (died as an infant)

On the sinister side of the pedestal are two female figures in Roman dress and that of a young boy standing between them. These are the 2 daughters of the Earl, Julia and Anne, who died aged 23 and 30, and the Earl's son Charles who died aged 12.

The monument is made entirely of marble, the sarcophagus, columns, arch of variously coloured marble and the 12 life sized figures of white marble

There is a long inscription in the centre of the base incised in roman lettering, capitals and lower case. The monument is enclosed by iron railings erected in 1755

The condition is good but the monument requires cleaning

MEMORIALS & MONUMENTS
Brasses

The fashion for brass rubbing has re-awakened interest in memorial brasses, many of which have survived in country churches in fine detail and represent an intriguing picture of the people they commemorate. Brasses were used for both secular and religious characters. All orders of the clergy received the tonsure and wore the same dress, except the Sexton. Certain orders carry a symbol:

Acolyte	candle
Exorcist	holy water pot
Lector	book
Sexton *(doorkeeper)*	key
Sub-deacon	basin and ewer

Many brasses have been lost, but the impression left on the slab in which they were set will give some idea of the brass it once held.
(see COSTUME: Arms and Armour)

Professors and Doctors of Law or Divinity wear vestments and their academic status is indicated by the skull cap tied beneath the chin and a long open robe with furred cape and hood. Widows who did not wish to re-marry retired to a convent and were known as vowesses.

Casement	slab into which a brass is set
Indent or matrix	mark left in casement by missing brass
Latten	alloy of copper and zinc with lead and tin used for brasses
Palimpsest	re-used brasses

1443 SIR WILLIAM COLWELL, w. & ch.

Floor, centre of S aisle
Two figures each 40 cm h.
Stone casement *(slab)* 94 x 44 cm overall
Group of 4 daus. below w. and 4 sons below knt.
4 shields of arms flanking canopy pinnacles
Black Letter marginal inscr. (worn), foot inscr. of two lines and prayer scrolls
Traces of enamelling on sword hilt and in shields
Bareheaded knt. on R in 15th century plate armour with hands conjoined, lion footrest, rowel spurs, skirt of lames, sword and dagger, no visible swordbelt
W. wears wide horned headdress and houpe lande; dog at foot
Crocketed and pinnacled double canopy with embattled entablature and pinnacled shafting
Symbols of 4 evangelists in roundels at corners of margin
Rebus in roundel in canopy above knt.'s head, a collet above a well

Recording note: *Record of brass memorials should include: position in church; component parts, noting whether relaid or palimpsest, missing parts (whether found elsewhere) and repairs; enamelling; measurements; description based on recognised format and abbreviations; description of canopy or border; heraldry; inscriptions in full including lettering style; description of merchant's marks; describe the slab, stone used and indents. Casements with indents. Casements with indents for missing brasses should also be recorded.*
Abbreviations acad. = academic dress; arm. = dressed in armour; civ. = in civilian dress; dau. = daughter; demi. = half effigy; fem. = female; frag. = fragment; inscr. = inscription; kng. = kneeling; knt. = knight; marg. = marginal; mur. = mural; mutil. = mutilated; pr. = priest; qd.pl. = quadrangular plate; R. = re-used (palimpsest) sm. = small (less than 45 cm); w. = wife; vv. = verses

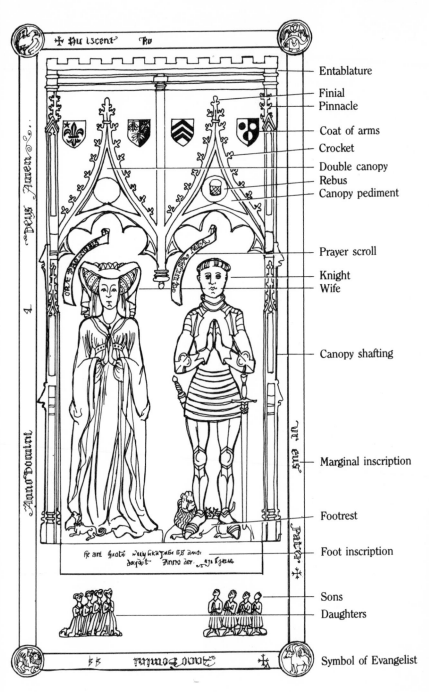

Entablature

Finial
Pinnacle

Coat of arms

Crocket

Double canopy
Rebus
Canopy pediment

Prayer scroll

Knight
Wife

Canopy shafting

Marginal inscription

Footrest

Foot inscription

Sons
Daughters

Symbol of Evangelist

MUSICAL INSTRUMENTS

Musical instruments appear in embroideries and tapestries, in stained glass and on tomb decoration. Actual instruments may be in use by the choir and there are few churches which do not have an organ.

STRINGED INSTRUMENTS PLAYED WITH BOW

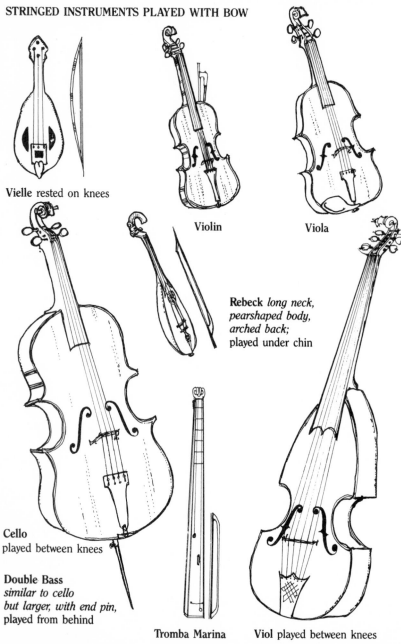

Vielle rested on knees

Violin

Viola

Rebeck *long neck, pearshaped body, arched back;* played under chin

Cello
played between knees

Double Bass
similar to cello
but larger, with end pin,
played from behind

Tromba Marina

Viol played between knees

PLUCKED INSTRUMENTS

Lute

Archlute or archiluth

Organistrum or hurdy gurdy played resting across knees of two players

Lyre

Irish harp or clairseach

Pedal harp
harp strings vertical to the soundboard

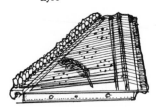

Psaltery *strings horizontal above soundboard*

Cittern
fig-shaped, 4/5 metal strings played with a plectrum

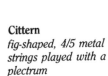

Mandoline	similar to lute: but with straight peg box, 4 pairs of metal strings
Guitar	figure of eight shaped

MUSICAL INSTRUMENTS

WIND INSTRUMENTS

Trumpet

Pitchpipe

Shawm
often played by goats
and grotesques

Serpent

Shofar
ram's horn trumpet played
in the Temple

Syrinx or panpipes

Tubo Cochleato

Tramba Spezzata

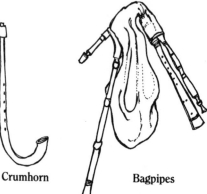

Crumhorn

Bagpipes

Vamphorn *(actual)* used for pitch
or *(decorative)* **trumpet** when
played by angels

Bassoon

MUSICAL INSTRUMENTS

WIND INSTRUMENTS

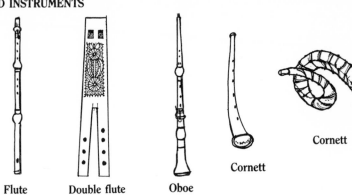

Flute   Double flute   Oboe

Cornett

Cornett

PERCUSSION

Drums   Handbells   Cymbals

Triangle with jingles   Tabor

MUSICAL INSTRUMENTS

KEYBOARD INSTRUMENTS

Cembalo Verticale

Positive organ *portative organs are small enough to carry*

Cottage Piano	small upright piano with iron frame introduced by John Isaac Hawkins in 1800. Other makers include Southwell, Robert Wornum, William Allen, Stodart, Alphaeus Babcock, Conrad Mayer and Jonas Chickening.
Electronic Organ	Small organ without pipes and keyboards of 5 octaves invented in 1840
Harmonium	electrically amplified organ the most popular made by Hammond
Pianola	automatic piano player driven by foot pedals played from perforated rolls, first appeared in 1842
Piano	either **grand** or **upright**. A trade label may give the name of the maker. The best known makers are Érard, Broadwood, Bechstein, Joseph Smith, Steinway, Silberman and Clementi.

ORGAN

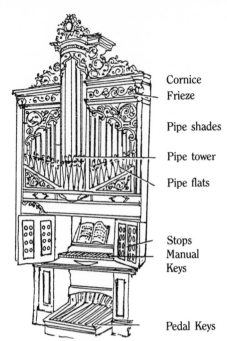

Cornice
Frieze

Pipe shades

Pipe tower

Pipe flats

Stops
Manual
Keys

Pedal Keys

The organ is usually the largest and often the most valuable piece of furniture in a church. Almost no pre-Reformation organs survive. Any musical instrument used before the advent of the organ will be rare and interesting.

British organ building reached its peak in the mid-19th century, co-inciding with a period of prosperity and devotion so that churches were equipped with many fine instruments in handsome cases. The leading builders were Hill, Willis, Gray, Davison and Walker. There were many local builders of note; good cases were designed by architects like Scott, Pearson, Bodley, Pugin and Dr Arthur Hill of the organ building firm.

Pipes
Except for painted front pipes organ pipes are usually made of zinc or lead. **Tin or pipe-metal** (a valuable alloy with a mottled appearance used only by organ makers) are most interesting. Some pipes, particularly large ones, may be wooden.

Action and soundboards
Organs of some age or good quality may have a **mechanical action** or tracker, where every action of the player has a direct mechanical effect. From 1880 to 1930, a **pneumatic action** was popular, whereby the player's actions are conveyed through the instrument by puffs of air. Pneumatic actions can be identified by the presence of a large amount of small bore lead tubing inside the lower parts of the case. Otherwise the action will be **electro-pneumatic**, where action is pneumatic but the pneumatic motors are started by small magnets or **direct electric**, where the action is by electric motors and solenoids.

The builder may be identified by a brass plate, but it may have been removed or replaced by a restorer's plate. Church organs may not have been new when installed.

MUSICAL INSTRUMENTS

Case	decorated in the same manner as furniture, made of furniture woods and sometimes topped with a cornice, pediment or other architectural feature
Console	where the player sits with at least one row of manual keys and usually a row of pedal keys. Note the lowest and highest notes of each,
	eg. CC-a (typical manual range)
	or CC-f (typical pedal range).
	If the lowest manual note is not C the organ is of early date or else a small compact positive organ from around 1900.
Decorated pipe shades	used to fill the space between the sloping line of the pipe tops and the rectangular frame of the case.
Flats	flat groups of pipes;
Keys	white keys will be of ivory, bone or ivorine (plastic); black keys of rosewood or ebony.
Pipes	may be decorated by contemporary painting (diapering).
Projecting wings	a legacy from early organs which had side doors to close when not in use.
Soundboards	contain the wind which blows the pipes and upon which the pipes stand.
Stops	each keyboard controls a group of stops, labelled in groups mounted in jambs, which will be set at different angles. Stops have engraved ivory or plastic heads indicating the tone and pitch they control.

The groups of stops are:

Great Organ	sole manual or the lower of two;
Swell Organ	upper manual;
Choir Organ	the lowest;
Solo Organ	above the swell in large organs; a fifth manual above the solo and very rare).
	Stops may be controlled by plastic tabs, usually set above the keyboards. There may be a central swell pedal or a trigger pedal at the side.
Towers	projecting groups of pipes (usually fewer and taller than flats)

Recording note: *Record detail of materials and appearance; maker's mark; any visible signs of repair and restoration; repairer's marks; any evidence of current maintenance (tuner's plate or notebook).*

Since the introduction of stained glass in the 12th century, many churches' chief glory is their windows. Windows are used to tell stories, explain texts, commemorate generosity or simply to decorate the church. Stained glass windows were often targets for the iconoclasts of the Reformation, but many fine early windows survive or mediaeval glass may be found put back haphazardly into windows by later restorers. In addition there are many marvellous Victorian and Edwardian windows, notably those of the Pre-Raphaelite Brotherhood, and a revival of the use of stained glass in 20th century churches.

Most commonly, windows show biblical scenes or the figures of saints. They may be costumed or wearing contemporary dress and are often surrounded by complex design and allegory. Colours are very rich, particularly in the late mediaeval period. The leading which links individual lights is not especially significant but the best view of the lead tracery of the window is from the outside looking in.

The scenes may include a variety of figures, animals and birds. In the 16th and 17th centuries these were mostly likely to have been taken directly from engravings in a series of well known contemporary source books.

Tempesta's translation of Ovid's Metamorphoses of 1606 was a popular source, birds were modelled from A Colleart's *Avium Vivae Icones;* fish from J Sadeler's *Piscium Vivae Icones;* flowers from Sadeler's *Florae Deae* or Crispin van de Passe's *Hortus Floridus (1614);* animals from Conrad Gessner's *Icones Animalium,* M Gerardo's *Animalium Quadrupedum* and Tempesta's *Fighting Animals.* Sources for figures were more varied but include Jost Amman's *Kunstbuchlein (1599)* and the prints of J Saenredam after *Goltzius (1569).*

Texts and inscriptions are usually biblical in origin, unless they commemorate a particular patron or event. It may be possible to find a signature or mark in one particular light of the window. Such a mark may have been made by the artist who painted the glass, the designer or the workshop where it was made up. Certain workshops used standard models of saints, angels, Roman soldiers, monograms and musical instruments.

Windows consist of four elements:
the architectural frame usually of stone which conformed to contemporary architectural style; the glass or lights; the leading; the scene or figure depicted. The glass itself can be of many different types: cathedral (obscured); antique; pressed; bottled; stained; painted.

Armatures	metal linking pieces of glass
Blind tracery	tracery with stone or brick infill rather than glass
Canopy	framework of turrets, niches, arcades, or foliage above or around the figures continued in the tracery
Cusp	projecting point where foils meet
Dedication	commemoration message for donor or event
Enamelling	method of grinding glass to a fine powder, mixing with a fusible liquid and applying to white glass from which it tends to flake. Common in 16th century.
Eyelets	smallest sections of tracery
Fillets	borders, particularly beaded borders popular in the 12th & 13th centuries and copied in the 19th
Grisaille	yellow, grey or brown monochromatic colouring used from 13th century (not to be confused with yellow stain) with a pattern.
Hachures	small shading lines

WINDOWS
Terms

Heraldic	arms often included in windows, particularly if donated *(see HERALDRY)*
Inscription	Memorial: to persons, family or group or **Commemorative**: of event or institution
Lights	sections of window divided by transoms or mullions
Lined out	drawing in black paint or enamel
Quarries	regular form of square or diamond shaped glass
Rose window	circular window shape with concentric rings of lights arranged like flower petals
Stained glass	common term for polychrome windows, but misleading since only yellow, in various shades, can be obtained by staining
Texts	quotations from Bible or other sources
Tracery	ornamentation formed by the branching of mullions in the upper part of a window
Tracery lights	sections of the ornamental tracery formed by the branching of mullions in the upper part of a window
Wheel window	circular window similar to rose window but with radiating tracery

Oriel when supported on corbels

Lucarne on a spire

Dormer on a house roof

Lunette
semi-circular window, panel or decoration

Eye, Oculus or **Oeil-de-Boeuf** round or oval window with radiating glazing bars

Wheel
window which has radiating tracery

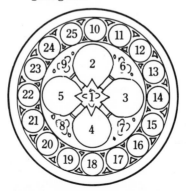

Rose
window which has concentric tracery

Recording note: *Windows should be numbered in the appropriate sequence as indicated.*

Window Heads

Norman

Lancet

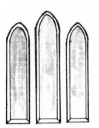

Grouped Lancets

Tracery

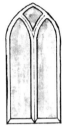

13th century
Y-tracery

13th century
Plate

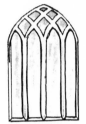

13th century
Intersected

13th century
Geometrical

13th and 14th century
Curvilinear or Flowing

14th century
Reticulated

14th century
Drop

14th century
Flamboyant

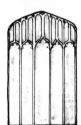

15th century
Rectilinear, Panel
or Perpendicular

223

WINDOWS
Terms

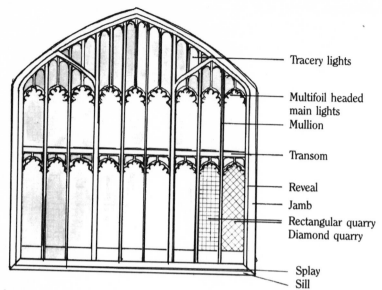

- Tracery lights
- Multifoil headed main lights
- Mullion
- Transom
- Reveal
- Jamb
- Rectangular quarry
- Diamond quarry
- Splay
- Sill

Window of 9 multifoiled lights, arranged in triplets in two stages within tracery of 15th century rectilinear form

Lights

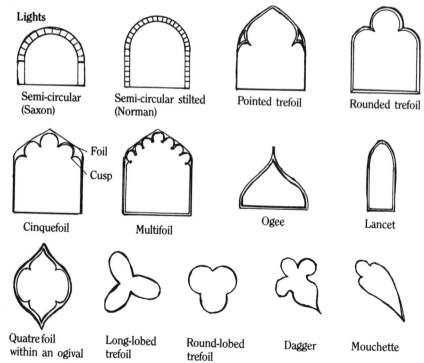

Semi-circular (Saxon)

Semi-circular stilted (Norman)

Pointed trefoil

Rounded trefoil

Cinquefoil — Foil, Cusp

Multifoil

Ogee

Lancet

Quatrefoil within an ogival

Long-lobed trefoil

Round-lobed trefoil

Dagger

Mouchette

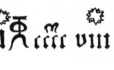

Thomas of
Oxford

Christopher Webb

Geoffrey Webb

John Thornton

Robert Hendra and
Geoffrey Harper

Paul Woodroffe

Powell & Sons
of Whitefriars

J E Nuttgens

pre-1910

post-1910

Francis Skeat

Francis Skeat

Charles Kempe

W Holland
Warwick

William
Warrington

M E Aldrich Rope

WINDOWS
Makers' Marks

Reginald Bell

Clayton & Bell

Thomas
Willement

John Clement Bell

Alfred Bell

M C Farrar Bell

William
Wailes

C C Townshend
& J Howson

Goddard & Gibbs

Rachel de
Montmorency

Hugh Easton

Horace
Wilkinson

J W Kubler

E F Brickdale

Edward Jenkins
Prest

226

H W Bryans

J N Comper

Martin Travers

T Salusbury

Martin Webb

John Lawson
(Goddard & Gibbs)

Peter Cole

Caroline Benyon

Percy Bacon & Bros.

Lawrence S Lee

pre-1970   post-1970
Wipple Mowbray Church Furnishing Ltd

Ray Bradley

Henry James Salisbury

N H J Westlake

Tom Carter Shapland

227

WINDOWS
17th century Window

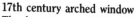

17th century arched window
The largest area of this light, as now assembled, is taken up by a series of rectangular pictures set in elaborate frames of ornamental strapwork and ranged in units of 6 or 8, each unit surmounted by shallow intersecting ogee arches squared up to make rectangular panels.

The arched head of the window has in the centre a coat of arms within a wreath of leaves and a rectangular frame. Surmounting and flanking it is a medley of disparate figures, birds, fish and other decorative devices, many incomplete, leaded up into a bizarre patchwork.
The pictorial panels are painted in brilliant colours and have a scrollwork setting.

The pattern of the leads is from **Walter Gede's** *Booke of Sundry Draughtes* (1615).
The painter of the panel made use of engravings for his subject matter, in some cases virtually the whole print was copied but in others only some small part was used.

Late 19th century window

Stonework is of the late 19th century with 3 trefoil headed lights with 14th century reticulated-style tracery.

1.	Dove descending amidst 3 stars in purple night sky
2 & 3.	Sprig of oak leaves with acorn in natural colouring against a light yellow ground.
4.	Crescent moon against dark blue sky.
5.	Sun against light blue sky.
6 & 7.	In each a trefoil lined out in black against a pale yellow ground.
8, 9 & 10.	In each 3 angels in white girdled tunics, the centre angels playing a musical instrument, rebeck, harp and tabor, the outer angels singing. Multicoloured wings.
11,12 & 13.	Text: "We have seen his star / in the East and are come / to worship him" Matthew chap. II v.2 Black 19th century gothic capitals and lower case on a pale yellow ground, difficult to read.
14.	3 shepherds, placed vertically, the top one standing, the lowest one kneeling, all with nomads' headdresses, each in a different brightly coloured cloak, red, yellow and blue; two hold crooks, the kneeling shepherd does not appear to.
15.	BVM (Blessed Virgin Mary) seated with infant Christ on knee and Joseph standing behind. BVM in royal blue mantle with gold trimming. Infant Christ swaddled. Joseph in dark red cloak. All nimbed in yellow.
16.	Magi (3) similarly placed to shepherds: Caspar in purple robe with fur cape-collar attached with a tied chain; Melchior in rich brown robe; Balthazar (youngest) kneeling in white tunic and emerald green super-tunic, with crown on the ground and bearing a gift. Plain silver dado behind all 3 scenes, with light blue sky above.
17 & 19.	A kneeling angel in each, both with flame coloured wings and nimbi, yellow stain ground.
18.	Old Testament Altar of Sacrifice in natural colours against a green ground.
20.	Artist's signature. Mark of a daisy within a bell: Margaret Bell.

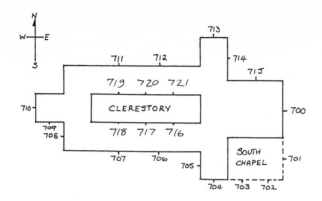

Recording Note:

Plan: *Windows should be recorded on a sketch plan of the church in a numbered sequence. Chapels should be described by compass point rather than name, i.e. South Chapel rather than Lady Chapel. Number the East window behind the altar 700 and work clockwise in arabic numerals, suffixing T for tower windows. Orientate the plan with a compass bearing.*

Window: *Record the shape and appearance of each window with a sketch or tracing of a photograph. Take the number of the window from the plan and record its position, i.e. 706 would be Nave S wall E; 720, Clerestory N wall centre.*

Lights: *Number the sketch plan to record the lights, across from left to right, starting at the top. Record each light in numerical sequence. Start with the tracery lights and move on to the main lights, dividing the later into sections, starting with the head, followed by the canopy, if any, then the subject, figures and background, then bottom panels and inscription or dedication. Note style of lettering. Identify figures and subjects. Describe colours in primary tones. Identify the tracery and makers' marks.*

Inside Churches can be no more than an introduction to the decoration and furnishings encountered in British churches. In each subject area there are many helpful secondary sources, some of which are recommended here. Some interesting primary sources may also be available through the incumbent of the parish or through county record offices. Recognised church recorders may also refer queries to various professionals through the National Association of Decorative and Fine Arts Societies.

General Reading

Addleshaw, G W O and Etchells, Frederick
The Architectural Setting of Anglican Worship
Faber and Faber, 1948

Anson, Peter
Fashions in Church Furnishings, 1840-1940
Faith Press, 1960

Betjeman, Sir John
Collins Guide to Parish Churches of England and Wales
Collins, 1980

Cox, Charles and Harvey, Alfred
English Church Furniture
E P Publishing, 1973

Curl, James Stevens
English Architecture: an illustrated glossary
David and Charles, 1977

Howkins, Christopher
Discovering Church Furniture
Shire Publications, 1980

Lewis, Philippa and Darley, Gillian
Dictionary of Ornament
Macmillan, 1986

Miller, Judith (ed.)
Miller's Pocket Antiques Fact File
Mitchell Beazley, 1988

Pevsner, Sir Nikolaus and others
The Buildings of England
Penguin

Randall, Gerald
Church Furnishing and Decoration in England and Wales
Batsford, 1980

Royal Commission on Historical Monuments, England
Inventories of historical monuments
HMSO

Stafford, Maureen and Ware, Dora
An Illustrated Dictionary of Ornament
Allen and Unwin, 1974

Oxford University
The Victoria History of the Counties of England
Press

Victoria and Albert Museum catalogue
Victorian Church Art
(November 1971-January 1972)

Architecture

Child, Mark
Discovering Church Architecture
Shire Publications, 1976

Council for British Archaeology
Recording a Church: an illustrated glossary
1988

Fletcher, Sir Bannister
History of Architecture
Athlone Press, 1975

Harries, J
Discovering Churches
Shire Publications, 1972

Harris, John and Lever, Jill
Illustrated glossary of architecture 850-1830
Faber and Faber, 1966

Attributes & Allegory

Child, Heather and Colles, Dorothy — Christian Symbols, Ancient and Modern
Bell and Hyman, 1971

Farmer, David Hugh — The Oxford Dictionary of Saints
Oxford University Press, 1978

Ellwood Post, W — Saints, Signs and Symbols
SPCK, 1964

Hall, James — Dictionary of Subjects and Symbols in Art
John Murray, 1987

Costume

Borg, A — Arms and Armour in Britain
HMSO, 1977

Blair, C — European and American Arms c. 1100-1850
Batsford 1962

Mayo, Janet — The History of Ecclesiastical Dress
Batsford, 1985

Cunnington, P — A Dictionary of English Costume
A and C Black 1960

Cunnington, P — Handbook of English Costume (various volumes)
Faber and Faber 1973

Yarwood, Doreen — English Costume from the 2nd Century BC to 1960
Batsford

Decoration

Brackett, O — English Furniture Illustrated
Hamlyn

Croft-Murray, Edward — Decorative Mural Painting in England, 1537-1837
Country Life, 1962

Croft-Murray, Edward — Decorative Painting in England, the 18th and 19th centuries
Country Life, 1970

Gloag, J — A Short Dictionary of Furniture
Allen and Unwin, 1952

Meyer, F S — Handbook of Ornament
Dover, 1957

Rouse, Clive — Discovering Wall Paintings
Shire Publications, 1980

Ware, D and Stafford, M — An Illustrated Dictionary of Ornament
Allen and Unwin, 1974

Heraldry

Burke, Sir John Bernard — The General Armory of England, Scotland, Ireland and Wales
Tabard, 1966

Fearn, Jacqueline — Discovering Heraldry
Shire Publications

Fox-Davies, A C — A Complete Guide to Heraldry
Nelson, 1969

Friar, Stephen	A New Dictionary of Heraldry
	Alpha Books
MacKinnon, Charles	The Observer Book of Heraldry
	Warne
Moncrieffe, Sir Iain and Pottinger, Don	Simple Heraldry Cheerfully Illustrated
	Nelson, 1952
Papworth, John Wood	Papworth's Ordinary of British Armorials
	Tabard, 1961
Summers, Peter	Hatchments in Britain (various volumes)
	Phillimore, 1974-1980

Lettering

Johnston, E	Writing and Illuminating and Lettering
	Pitman, 1906

Ceramics

Barnard, Julian	Victorian Ceramic Tiles
	Studio Vista, 1972
Cushion, J P and Honey, W B	A Handbook of Pottery and Porcelain Marks
	Faber and Faber
Eames, Elizabeth S	Mediaeval Tiles: a handbook
	British Museum, 1968
Hughes, G Bernard	The Country Life Collectors' Pocket Book

Metal

Banister, Judith	English Silver Hallmarks
	Foulsham, 1970
Camp, John	Discovering Bells and Bellringing
	Shire Publications, 1975
Cotterell, Howard Herschel	Old Pewter, its makers and marks
	C E Tuttle, 1963
Hollister-Short, G J	Discovering Wrought Iron
	Shire Publications, 1970
Oman, Charles	English Church Plate
	Oxford University Press, 1957
Peal, Christopher	British pewter and Britannia metal
	John Gifford, 1971
Walters, H B	Church Bells of England
	Oxford University Press, 1977

Paper

Briquet, Charles M	Les Filigranes
	Paris, 1907
Darley, L.S.	Introduction to Book Binding
	Faber and Faber, 1965
Heawood, Edward	Watermarks etc
	1950
Tate, W E	The Parish Chest: A Study of the Records of Parochial Administration in England
	Cambridge University Press, 1969

Stone

Kilburn, Father E	A Walk around the Church of the London Oratory
	Sand and Co, 1966

Textiles

Kelly, Francis and Schwabe, Randolph — A Short History of Costume and Armour, 1066-1800
David and Charles, 1972

Dean, Beryl — Ecclesiastical Embroidery
Batsford, 1958

Fokker, Nicolas — Persian and Other Oriental Carpets for Today
Allen and Unwin, 1973

Hands, M H — Church Needlework
Faith Press, 1957

Wood

Corkhill, Thomas — A Glossary of Wood
Stobart and Sons, 1984

Edwards, R — A Shorter Dictionary of English Furniture
Hamlyn, 1964

Gloag, J — A Short Dictionary of Furniture
Allen and Unwin, 1952

Hayward, C H — English Period Furniture
Evans, 1971

Jervis, Simon — The Woodwork of Winchester Cathedral
Friends of Winchester Cathedral, 1976

Joy, E T — The Country Life Book of Chairs
Hamlyn, 1967

Smith, J C D — A Guide to Church Woodcarving: misericords and bench-ends
David and Charles, 1974

Smith, J C D — Church Woodcarvings: A West Country Study
David and Charles, 1969

Clocks

Baillie, G Hand Loomes, J — Watchmakers and Clockmakers of the World
NAG Press, 1976

Beeson, C F C — English Church Clocks, 1280-1850
Phillimore, 1971

Betts, J — The National Trust Pocket Guide to Clocks
Octopus Books, 1985

Loomes, B — Watchmakers and Clockmakers of the World
NAG Press, 1976

Rose, R E — English Dial Clocks
Antique Collectors Club, 1978

Smith, A — Clocks and Watches
1975

Memorials & Monuments

Chapman, Leigh — Brasses and Brass Rubbing
Shire Publications, 1987

Greenhill, Frank — Incised Effigal Slabs
Faber and Faber, 1976

Kemp, Brian — English Church Monuments
Batsford, 1980

Macklin, H W — The Brasses of England
E P Group. 1975

Mill Stephenson, B A	A List of Monumental Brasses in the British Isles *Headley, 1926*
Norris, Malcolm	Monumental Brasses: the Craft *Faber and Faber, 1978*
Norris, Malcolm	Monumental Brasses: the Memorials *Phillips and Page, 1989*
Stone, Lawrence	Sculpture in Britain: the Middle Ages *Penguin, 1955*
Tummers H A	Early Secular Effigies in England: the Thirteenth Century *Brill, 1980*
Whinney, Margaret	Sculpture in Britain: 1530-1830 *Penguin, 1964*

Musical Instruments

Clutton, C and Niland, A	The British Organ *Batsford, 1963*
Hindley, G	Musical Instruments *Hamlyn, 1971*

Windows

Lee, Lawrence, Seddon, George and Stephens, Francis	Stained Glass *Mitchell Beazley, 1976*
Sewter, A Charles	The Stained Glass of William Morris and his Circle *Yale University Press, 1974-5*
Harrison, K	An Illustrated Guide to the Windows of King's College Chapel, Cambridge
Harrison, Martin	Victorian Stained Glass *Barrie and Jenkins, 1980*
Harries, John	Discovering Stained Glass *Shire Publications, 1980*
Kirkby, H T	The Stained Glass Artist *British Society of Master Glass Painters' Journal Vol X, No 4* *1950-51*

INDEX

INDEX
The explanation of a proper name or term is given on pages with highlighted numbers in the index.

INDEX

INDEX

Tex - Zoo